SHALOM

FOR THE HEART

SHALOM
FOR THE HEART

~~~~~~~~~~~~~~~~~~~~~~~~~~~~~~~~

TORAH-INSPIRED DEVOTIONS
for A SACRED LIFE

RABBI EVAN MOFFIC

To Sylvia,
with
Blessings

Evan M

ABINGDON PRESS
NASHVILLE

SHALOM FOR THE HEART
TORAH-INSPIRED DEVOTIONS FOR A SACRED LIFE

Copyright © 2016 by Evan Moffic

Library of Congress Cataloging-in-Publication Data has been requested.

ISBN 978-1-5018-2737-2

16 17 18 19 20 21 22 23—10 9 8 7 6 5 4 3 2 1

MANUFACTURED IN THE UNITED STATES OF AMERICA

Contents

Foreword

Igrew up as a pastor's daughter in a nondenominational church outside Chicago—a church that began in a movie theater, not particularly traditional in terms of style and practice. When I attended a Christian college in Southern California, I focused my literature study (for reasons I can't really even remember now) on Judaism, Jewish poetry and philosophy, and particularly Holocaust literature and modern Jewish fiction. Another way to say it: this Christian Midwestern girl found herself sitting in a library carrel, looking out at the Pacific Ocean; and in that place she found her faith and her soul awakened by Noah benShea, Chaim Potok, Aharon Appelfeld, Cynthia Ozick, Saul Bellow, Philip Roth, and Abraham Heschel, among others.

Fast forward a decade: I found myself as a part of a church in Grand Rapids, Michigan, that believed the Jewish roots of our Christian faith were fundamental and that they deserved study and attention. Many in our congregation studied Hebrew, and we joked that if you looked through the name tags of the children in our Sunday school, you might think you'd traveled back to the Old Testament. For decades Christians have been naming their children Mary and Joseph and John. But this nursery was packed with Esthers and Miriams and Naomis, Ashers and Shaloms.

All that to say, I'm a Christian who loves Judaism, who learns from it, connects deeply with it, and has had my own faith and practice deepened and challenged by the Jewish faith and tradition. And I'm so very thankful for the professors and teachers and pastors and rabbis who introduced me to this wonderful faith tradition.

I'm so thankful that Rabbi Moffic has visited our community to teach us about Sabbath—something that Christians have largely regarded as an optional practice, something about which the Jewish community has much to teach us. And when Rabbi Moffic invited our community to a Shabbat service, the warmth of his congregation was palpable, and we were thankful for their welcome.

I wish that every Christian I know could sit around a table at an Indian restaurant with Rabbi Moffic and his wife, Ari—also a rabbi. My husband, Aaron, and I have treasured the time we've spent around the table with them—they're wise and kind and funny, and the depth and richness of their faith bleeds into every conversation. But since that kind of lunch schedule would tax the Rabbis Moffic beyond reason, the next best thing is this book.

Most Christians—myself certainly included—have so much to learn from the Jewish tradition and the study of the Torah, and from Judaism's respect for the law and its value on ritual and connection within their community. My faith has been enriched tremendously by my study of Jewish philosophy, poetry, and fiction, and even more so by my friendships with Jewish scholars and theologians, the Moffics included.

This book is a gift for every Christian, anchoring us to a beautiful shared history that can deepen and enrich our understanding and our faith.

Shauna Niequist, best-selling author and speaker

Introduction

One Friday evening, the confirmation class of a neighboring Methodist church was visiting my synagogue. We began the service in the traditional way, with some Hebrew prayers and a few songs. As I looked out nervously, these confirmation students seemed bored and disengaged. Quite frankly, some of my own students at the synagogue looked the same. Then I approached the ark—the holiest place in the Jewish sanctuary, the place where we keep the scrolls of parchment with the Hebrew words of the Torah (the Five Books of Moses) written upon them.

I lifted one of the scrolls and took it out. I then asked a few of the students to help me unwrap the scroll. As we did so, the students slowly formed a circle, with each one grasping part of the parchment. Their eyes began to light up. They started surveying the parchment. They pointed at blocks of Hebrew text, asked questions, turned and exclaimed surprise to one another. Questions poured out. Who wrote the Torah? How can you read these words? Has anyone ever read the whole thing? Why is there a big space here? Where are the Ten Commandments?

The Word of God had come alive for these students. An ancient text sparked questions, interest, and excitement. An ancient scroll felt startlingly relevant. That is the moment this book began.

WHY TORAH MATTERS

For millennia Jews have called the Torah the Tree of Life. For Jews it is God incarnate in words. Through those words we glean our beliefs, our practices, our history, our values. Our lives are spent climbing that tree, bringing us closer to God, and firmly rooting us in the soil of our ancestors.

For Christians, however, Torah has largely been unknown or ignored. Even the word *Torah* has been replaced by "Old Testament" or "Jewish Bible" or "Hebrew Scripture." None of these descriptions are wrong. But Jesus lived by and studied *the Torah*. He embraced it as the Tree of Life.

As it did for all Jews of his time, Torah guided Jesus's daily practices and shaped his stories and teachings. Jesus quoted Torah throughout the Gospels, and Paul studied it and cited it frequently throughout his letters. When Jesus said, "I did not come to abolish the law but to fulfill it," He was not rejecting the Torah; he was demonstrating its significance. The words *law* and *Torah* are the same in the Greek. To fulfill the Torah is not to reject it. It is to live by it and to make it a source of truth and guidance.

We live in an era of rapid change. Popular ancestry websites remind us that we know ourselves better—we find greater stability in a fast-moving world—when we have a firmer grasp of our roots. Christianity is rooted in Judaism, and Judaism is rooted in the Torah. To discover our roots is to better understand ourselves and the reason God put us here.

Torah is not for Jews only. The early Jewish sages said God wrote the Torah in seventy languages. The Torah speaks to us in the language of our own faith and traditions. The more languages in which we can speak it, the more we can fulfill it.

WHY A RABBI WROTE THIS BOOK

Can a rabbi teach Christians from and about Torah today? If my experience with the confirmation students is any indication, the answer is an unequivocal yes. The Torah is not only for Jews, and God's book makes its word accessible and meaningful for Christians today. I chose to teach Torah through a book of devotions because these words are meant for the heart. Whenever I open a book and study Torah, I feel God's presence—what some call the Holy Spirit—dwelling before me. I yearn to share that presence, and I have seen the way it can speak to people of all faiths.

In 2011, I spent a year studying Torah with a Christian minister, and it enriched his preaching and understanding of Jesus's parables. A Christian student later described to me that, after she studied Torah, she visited the Holy Land with a new set of eyes and tools for understanding what the Promised Land meant for Jesus and the disciples. Torah is not something Jesus transcended; it is the heritage imbuing his teaching, and it can shape the lives of all of us today.

I've witnessed this truth during lectures I've delivered at dozens of churches, from evangelical Southern Baptist to liberal United Church of Christ. Invariably someone asks what Jews believe about Jesus. I wrote a whole book addressing that question, but this book offers up another perspective.

In Judaism Torah is God brought down to earth. *Torah is God as revealed through words. We study the words of Torah so as to conform our lives to God's will.* Therefore, by studying the Torah, we will not only experience the intellectual and spiritual world of Jesus in the first century and glean insights and truths for our own deepening relationship with God but also discover a new lens for seeing God's presence in our lives today.

HOW THIS BOOK IS ORGANIZED

Two thousand years ago a group of rabbis divided the Five Books of Moses into fifty-four sections. These sections are known as the "Torah portions." The Torah portion schedule is the Jewish lectionary. It differs from the Christian lectionary in that its readings come only from the Five Books of Moses. On every Sabbath, the weekly Torah portion is read aloud from a Torah scroll. The rabbi then delivers a sermon based on the verses read. The guiding principle is that the Torah verses contain timeless truths we can apply in our lives today.

This book consists of devotions for each of the Torah portions in the first two books of Moses (Genesis and Exodus). I have chosen short verses from each Torah portion and sought to choose ones that may not be very well-known. Each verse is the springboard for a devotion and truth we can bring into our lives.

SHALOM

FOR THE HEART

Bereshit: Genesis 1:1–6:8

Beginnings

In the beginning God created the heavens and the earth.
(Genesis 1:1 NKJV)

I am a runner. I run several miles each day, and on most days, the hardest part of my run—the time when my feet drag and my mind tells me I should still be in bed—is the beginning: the first mile or two. That's when I'm feeling the most resistance. That's when I want to quit.

After a while, however, a feeling of flow kicks in. The strides become more natural. My mind begins to wander, and I enjoy the scenery. Breathing comes regularly and easily.

On the face of it, this pattern seems counterintuitive. Shouldn't energy be highest at the beginning and diminish as the run continues? What is happening?

The Energy of Breath

The act of beginning produced an energy of its own. When God spoke and the world came into being, an energy was introduced into creation. The Torah calls this energy *Ruach Elohim*, the spirit of God.

This spirit of God with which the earth began does not diminish. It is the very breath of life. We feel it when we breathe. We feel it when we pray.

The Hebrew word for breath is *neshimah*, which is also the word for soul. *Within our souls is the very breath of God.* The energy with which the world was created lives on within us.

A BEGINNING THAT DOES NOT END

We need that energy because beginnings are hard. Do you remember the fear, the tingling, when you last began a new relationship, a new job, a new adventure? Did the fear ever feel like too much? Did you ever want to stop, to withdraw, to put your head back under the pillow?

But imagine if God had simply stopped at the beginning. There would be no world, no humanity, no opportunity for our own beginnings.

The great Rabbi Nachman of Bratslav, from the eighteenth century, said the world is a very narrow bridge, and the most important part of crossing that bridge is not to be afraid. Beginnings may make us afraid, but once we begin, the fear subsides. Energy builds up. We develop momentum. That is when a beginning becomes a blessing and we cross the bridge linking us to God and to another.

Eternal God,
May you fill my beginnings with blessings, and may you bless me with many more beginnings than endings. Amen.

The Voice

> Some time later, Cain presented an offering to the Lord from the land's crops while Abel presented his flock's oldest offspring with their fat. The Lord looked favorably on Abel and his sacrifice but didn't look favorably on Cain and his sacrifice. (Genesis 4:3-5)

My oldest daughter loves the show *The Voice*. Sometimes she coaxes me into watching it with her. I confess I am not a big fan of the music. I am always intrigued, however, by one part of the show—the most difficult, emotional part—the time when the judges have to tell one of the losing contestants he or she did not make it.

Typically the dueling contestants are both talented. Often they have trained together, having both made it past some of the initial rounds. Only one of them, however, can move onto the next round.

Each of the judges has a different style for informing the losing performer, but all convey the same message: It's not about failure. It's not about a lack of talent. It's simply the reality that a choice must be made and that the winner fits what the judge is seeking for the next round. In other words, one person must lose this round, but he or she is not a loser.

WHAT CAIN MISSES

I wish Cain had been able to hear this message back in Genesis 3. He and Abel had both made an offering to God. For an unspecified reason, God preferred Abel's. God knew Cain was angry, saying to him, "sin is crouching at the door" (Genesis 4:7 ESV). Still angry and frustrated, Cain ignored the warning and murdered his brother.

It didn't have to turn out that way. God's preference was not an indictment of Cain. As we learn later, Cain went on to become the builder of the first city. Yet his reaction echoes throughout history.

TO COMPARE IS TO DESPAIR

We compare ourselves to others, and when another is preferred, we take it as a personal failure. Competition can bring out our best, but too often, it also brings out our worst.

A later Jewish legend suggests Cain ultimately repented for his sin and God accepted it. Cain's forgiveness thus became an example of God's infinite grace. If God can forgive Cain, God can forgive us. Cain's repentance reminds us that the door is always open to forgiveness and redemption.

God,
Our society labels people as winners and losers. Yet I know that in your eyes I am sacred and unique, blessed with gifts. May I be open to growing and changing with your love. Amen.

A Day from Heaven

God blessed the seventh day and made it holy, because on it God rested
from all the work of creation. (Genesis 2:3)

An admirer once asked the great pianist Vladimir Horowitz how he
could play so beautifully. He answered, "The notes—anyone can play.
But the pause between the notes...ah...that is where the music lies."
What Horowitz said about music is also true about our lives. It is in the
pauses—the rests, the spaces in between—that meaning is made and that
holiness is felt.

This idea feels so counterintuitive today. We are always doing, always
moving, always on call. A 2014 survey showed we now drink more instant
coffee than at any time in American history. But that's not the way God
created us. It's not the way God created the world. God worked, then rested.
God created, then paused.

The first Sabbath was not only the completion of creation but also the
culmination of creation. Thus, our Sabbath is the day when we can marvel at
the beauty of the world God created. It is the day we enjoy what the ancient
sages called "a taste of heaven." It is a day when we stop thinking about the
what of life and remind ourselves of the *why* of life.

START SMALL

For those of us who struggle to keep the Sabbath, it helps to start small.
We do not need to follow the ancient Jewish practice of refraining from all

work for a full twenty-four hours. We do not need to disconnect completely from the world. We can light candles. We can go for a walk with our spouse or a friend. We can call a friend we haven't spoken with in a while.

The point of the Sabbath is not only to rest; it is to sanctify. It is to lift us out of the physical realm and glimpse the beauty of the spiritual. It is the place, as one rabbi put it, where heaven and earth meet.

And we can visit that place every week.

Eternal God,
You rested on the seventh day. Give me the strength of spirit to do the same. Give me the wisdom to stop doing and start being. Amen.

Noach: Genesis 6:9–11:32

God Enough

Noah was a righteous man, blameless in his generation. Noah walked with God. (Genesis 6:9 ESV)

When I was eighteen I became a counselor at a summer camp for boys. I had grown up attending the camp for eight weeks every summer. It was a second home.

After a week adjusting to life as a counselor rather than a camper, I started to thrive. I loved leading the tennis program, being in a cabin with the youngest and newest kids at camp, and bonding with the other counselors. When I sat down with the camp director for my end of the year review, I got ready for some great news. Counselors typically got a small bonus if they did well, and I was anticipating a stellar evaluation and nice bonus.

The director began by talking about the wonderful things kids and parents had to say about me. He talked about my solid leadership of the tennis program. Then he said I was a "good counselor." Then he stopped talking.

I was waiting. I kept waiting. Then I said in a questioning voice, "Good counselor?" "Yes," he said, "a good counselor."

"Well, wasn't I a great counselor?" I stammered.

"Sometimes," he said, "it's OK to be good enough."

I left the meeting upset, even angry. I later came to see he was right. I was not a great counselor, but that's OK. Sometimes we simply need to be "good enough."

In doing so, we follow in the footsteps of Noah. The ancient rabbis were careful readers of the biblical text. They noticed God describes Noah as "a righteous man blameless in his generation." His generation was wicked. That's why God sent the flood.

In another generation, Noah wouldn't have been considered so righteous. Indeed, he did not speak to God face to face, as Moses did. He did not start a new religion, as Abraham did.

But Noah was "good enough." He listened to God and followed God's instructions. He gave humanity an opportunity to be reborn and start over. He walked with God.

Eternal Source of Life,
I am not perfect. I do not live a perfect life. But You do not ask for perfection. You ask me to walk with You in grace and goodness, and Your grace is good enough for me. Amen.

Spirit vs. Flesh

> The end of all flesh has come before Me, for the earth is filled with violence through them; and behold, I will destroy them with the earth.
>
> (Genesis 6:13 NKJV)

With these haunting words God tells Noah of the upcoming destruction of the earth. The violence has become too great. Humanity has become like the teenagers immortalized in *Lord of the Flies*. Violence and power rule the day.

As we look around our world, we may think that not much has changed. Violence still plagues many parts of the world. Yet, according to many social scientists and historians, violence has declined significantly over the centuries! With the rise of global trade and travel, we are slowly realizing, as Abraham Lincoln and the title of a more recent book by Harvard scholar Steven Pinker put it, the "better angels of our nature."

A DIFFERENT KIND OF VIOLENCE

But violence is not always physical. Jewish commentators draw a parallel between the physical violence of Noah's time and material desires of our own.

They compare the Bible's description in this verse to a large group of people arriving at a banquet hall. Soon they start fighting over the food. The fight descends into a massive brawl of greed and anger. The host then arrives and clears the banquet table. "With an empty table," he reasons, "there is nothing left to fight over."

WHAT NOAH KNEW

The message? So often, *our greed leads to emptiness. We fight over what is in front of us only to lose what is inside of us.* We confuse our material desires with our spiritual needs, believing that one can satisfy the other, and thereby lose both.

What made Noah unique, according to the Jewish sages, was that he "walked with God" (Genesis 6:9). He made the spiritual part of his being primary; he knew God was with him always. He did not ignore his material needs—indeed, he built an ark and housed the animals and had to feed and sustain them—but he never lost sight of the God who walked alongside him. So must we.

God of the Universe,
Remind me that You walk beside me so that I may always remember
that I walk alongside You. Amen.

The First Step

It rained on the earth forty days and forty nights. That same day
Noah…went into the ark. (Genesis 7:12-13)

A couple came in to see me. Their son had been out of college for a year.
He had done well there, yet he could not find a job. He was living with
his parents and sleeping in his old room.

This situation is not uncommon. But what they said to me—and what
I have heard from parents in similar circumstances—was more concerning.
His situation had paralyzed him. Even though he knew he should be looking for a job, he seemed to have given up. He did not want to get out of bed,
and when he did, he did not want to get off the couch. His ambition and
excitement had morphed into cynicism and anger.

WAITING WITHOUT ACTING

Life can do that to us sometimes. Even our biblical heroes experienced
these moments. The Jewish sages, drawing from the awkward wording of
our Torah verse, tell us Noah hesitated before entering the ark. Even though
he had been building it for 120 years, he did not enter it when the storm
started.

He reasoned, "God has spared me thus far. If I am such a righteous man,
God will let me live through the rain." It was only after days had passed and
the water had reached his ankles that Noah finally called for his family and
the animals and entered into the ark.

What was he thinking? Like the young man whose parents came to see me, he probably felt he was going to drown with the rest of the world. He felt helpless and hopeless. Only imminent danger forced him to think differently.

START SMALL, AND WE'LL END BIG

We cannot always control our circumstances, but we can control how we respond to them. I told the parents to remind their son of who he is and how much he has achieved and can continue to achieve. I reminded them of an old Hebrew saying—one good act leads to another good act.

In other words, when we succeed in one thing, we develop the momentum to do more. Start small, and we'll end big. Taking that first step will not always be easy, but like Noah, it may save our lives.

God,
I don't need to wait to turn to You. I do not need to feel danger in order to feel Your presence. Remind me that You are guiding and sustaining me all along. Amen.

LECH-LECHA: GENESIS 12:1–17:27

The Comfort Zone

Go from your country and your kindred and your father's house to the land that I will show you. (Genesis 12:1 ESV)

When my oldest daughter learned to swim, she had a pretty easy time. She got the strokes, the kicking, the breathing. One part, however, kept eluding her. She couldn't float.

At first I was puzzled. Isn't floating the easy part? It seems to take much less effort than doing the crawl or backstroke. Then my wife gave me a short essay called "Floating Takes Faith," by Rabbi David Wolpe. Rabbi Wolpe pointed out that floating is hard because we give up control. We need to let our bodies go and rely on the water to hold us up. When we give up control, we leave our comfort zone. But that's when all the important stuff happens.

When God called on Abram to leave his father's house and journey to "the land that I will show you," God did not provide much detail. God did not pull out a map or a GPS to show Abram and Sarai the way. They had to step out from what was familiar and enter the unknown.

Sometimes, like Abram and Sarai, we choose to step outside our comfort zone. Other times—when a loved one dies, when we lose a job, when a cherished relationship ends—we are forced outside of it. We do not know how it will turn out. We cannot plan out every twist and turn. In fact, if we try to do so, we may close off options we will need along the way.

What matters most is our trust in the final destination. Our footsteps may falter, but God will not let us fall. When we trust in the final destination, new paths open up before us. It has been said that when we do not know where we are going, any path will do. Conversely, when we know where we are going, many paths can get us there.

I knew my daughter would learn to float. I didn't know it would take months, but I knew she had the courage to enter into the unknown. So do we.

God,
You call me out of my comfort zone. You illuminate the path before me and give me the strength and will to walk ahead. Amen.

Control

Lot chose for himself the entire Jordan Valley. Lot set out toward the east, and they separated from each other. (Genesis 13:11)

The late great Yogi Berra famously said, "If you come to a fork in the road, take it." The not-so-subtle point of Yogi's saying was that we sometimes overthink our decisions. Sometimes we just need to make a choice and stick with it. Unfortunately, making the wrong choice can get us in trouble. And the more trouble it causes, the harder it is to turn back.

Among the most searing illustrations of this truth is Lot. He and his uncle Abram have come to a fork in the road and have decided to go their separate ways. Lot chooses to go toward the Jordan Valley, the land of Sodom and Gomorrah. It promises comfort and riches.

Abram goes the opposite way. We know what happens next. Abram (now Abraham) has to rescue Lot and his family when God decides to destroy Sodom on account of its wickedness and immorality.

What made Lot choose to go to Sodom? Was he simply greedy? Was he unaware of its immorality and destructive culture, or did he simply not care?

Perhaps Lot suffered from what sometimes afflicts all of us. *The grass always looks greener on the other side.* Sodom was like the new job with a higher salary and bigger office, except we are not sure about the culture of the company. Sodom was like the bigger, fancier house, except we would be using up most of our savings to get it.

"All streams flow to the sea," says the Book of Ecclesiastes, "but the sea is never full" (1:7). Our desires are not fully satisfied.

The challenge, however, is not to eliminate our desires; it is to master them. That is the path of Abraham. Abraham always controls his desires, even when such control borders on the extreme. He controls his desire to reach out and protect his son when God calls upon him to sacrifice Isaac on the mountain. He controls his desire to let the residents of Sodom and Gomorrah perish instantly when he demands they receive a just hearing before God.

No one—not even our biblical heroes—is free from desires. What our heroes can teach us, however, is how to master them. Lot let his desires master him. By following God's ways, Abraham learned to master them.

God,
You made me a bundle of desires. But within them You placed Your spirit and guiding hand, leading me toward a life of holiness. Amen.

Givers and Takers

The LORD said to Abram, "...I will bless those who bless you."
(Genesis 12:1, 3)

Sometimes the Bible shatters conventional wisdom. It looks at our assumptions and turns them on their heads. This is one of those times.

On the surface, this verse seems straightforward. God is promising blessings to those who bless Abram, his tribe, and their descendants. Those who bless Israel will themselves be blessed.

Perhaps we are so accustomed to this verse that we forget how revolutionary it was. In the ancient Near East, tribes competed with one another. They competed over land, resources, and power. Even their gods competed. We associate the word *tribalism* with this kind of insularity and conflict. To be tribal is to focus on our own interests and self-preservation.

The God of Abraham offers a different vision. Tribes prosper when they bless others. God bestows blessings not on those who look out for themselves; *God blesses those who move beyond themselves.* God calls us to generosity rather than selfishness and promises that in the end, generosity benefits the giver.

WE TAKE WHEN WE GIVE

Perhaps you have volunteered at a soup kitchen or a school and felt you got much more than you gave. Perhaps you have supported an organization and felt uplifted by it. Well, you do not need to trust only your feelings. Science backs them up.

Wharton Professor Adam Grant wrote a wonderful book in 2013 called *Givers and Takers: A Revolutionary Approach to Success*. What he found is that people who give to others and to causes without expecting anything in return attain the highest levels of success.

Here's why: Takers, as the name suggests, are always trying to get something from you. Givers, in contrast, seek to help. The value they provide leads them to develop relationships that make for success.

What does this mean for your spiritual life? Give to your church without expecting some type of special favor from God. Give to your community without expecting some business connections in return. You might find such giving creates rewards you never imagined.

God,
Make me a vehicle for Your blessings. May they flow in and through me, giving light and life to the world. Amen.

Vayeira: Genesis 18:1–22:24

Hospitality: The Difference Between Life and Death

As soon as [Abraham] saw them, he ran from his tent entrance to greet them and bowed deeply. (Genesis 18:2)

Have you ever met with individuals and sensed they were not really listening? Perhaps they were distracted. Perhaps they were not interested. Maybe they even answered their phone and started talking, leaving you waiting and wondering. I bet you felt turned off.

Now think of someone who instantly made you feel at home. The moment you saw him or her, you had that person's full attention. A phone could ring, a person could walk by, but the attention remained focused on you. You probably felt close to that person.

The biblical Abraham was that kind of person. When you were with him, you had his full attention. No one was more important than the person in front of him, even God! We see a stunning example of his character in the opening words of this Torah reading.

God has appeared to Abraham. Then three men approach the tent where Abraham is standing, communing with God. But Abraham ends this communion and immediately tends to the guests in front of him. Not even a call from God could distract Abraham from his guests.

The Jewish sages looked to this incident as a model of hospitality. While we may think about hospitality purely in social terms, it was, in biblical times, the difference between life and death. Whenever weary travelers came to the door, a host could either prey upon them or nourish them. Abraham does the latter. He welcomes the strangers, feeds them, and washes their feet. Little does he know they are angels who were there to deliver him a message: his long-awaited son will soon arrive.

The lesson to draw from this story is not only that we may be, as the Book of Hebrews puts it, entertaining "angels unawares" (13:2 ESV). It is that *hospitality opens us up to God's presence everywhere.*

Putting away our cell phones and looking someone in the eye are not just good manners. They are sacred duties, because God is not only above us but around us, present in those we welcome and honor. When we honor the image of God in others, we honor the God who created us all.

God,
Open me up to what is in front of me without distraction, and let me give my attention to what should have my attention. Amen.

What Angels Can't Do

Abraham looked up and saw three men standing nearby. When he saw them, he hurried from the entrance of his tent to meet them and bowed low to the ground. (Genesis 18:2)

Reverend Martin Copenhaver relates an encounter between two members of his church in line at a convenience store. One said to the other, "Hey, didn't I wash your feet on Sunday night?"

"Yes, that was me. I thought I recognized you. But it was quite dark at the time, so I wasn't sure."

"Yeah, and I was a little nervous because I'd never done anything like that before. Let me introduce myself..."

Evidently, the face of the attendant behind the counter began to turn red, and the two finally realized how awkward their conversation seemed.[1]

Yet, it would not have seemed awkward four thousand years ago. Among the first things we see Abraham do when three visitors arrive at his tent is bring water to wash their feet. This conveys not only humility but also hospitality. It also lifts Abraham up, bringing him closer to God.

One of the great rabbinic sages of the nineteenth century taught this truth by looking at the language in the biblical text. In Genesis 18:2, the Hebrew translation can be read to say that the men are "standing above" Abraham. In Genesis 18:8, after he has welcomed and served them a meal, Abraham, according to another reading of the Hebrew translation, "stands above" them. (The Hebrew suffix for "nearby" can also be read as "above.")

What accounts for the change? As the Jewish interpreters put it, "at first, the visitors were higher than Abraham because they were angels and he a mere human being. But when he gave them food and drink and shelter, he stood even higher than the angels."

When we satisfy another's needs, we do more than even angels can do; we do what only people can do. Sometimes, as people of faith, we are too much like the angels. We would rather meditate than wash another's person's feet.

Yet, as the nineteenth-century rabbi Israel Salanter put it, "Most of us worry about our own bellies, and other people's souls, when we all ought to be worried about our own souls, and other people's bellies." To that we can only say amen.

God of all people,
Help me play the role of servant throughout my life, in love and with humility. Amen.

When It Is Right to Be Wrong

Then the Lord said, "Shall I hide from Abraham what I am about to do.... For I have chosen him, so that he will direct his children and his household after him to keep the way of the Lord by doing what is right and just." (Genesis 18: 17, 19)

When I began to serve my first congregation, a rabbinic mentor shared some wisdom with me. "Sometimes," he said, "when it comes to important matters within the synagogue, you will not get your way. The board or your president will make a decision you do not like. Just remember two things: either you did not make a good enough case for your position, or you are wrong."

Having been a rabbi now for ten years, I would add a third part to his words. Sometimes, being wrong can be a gift. *Sometimes, we learn more when we are wrong than when we are right.*

Abraham may well have felt this way after his argument with God over the fates of Sodom and Gomorrah. God has decided to destroy the two cities on account of their moral wickedness. Then Abraham rises up to challenge God.

ABRAHAM'S CHALLENGE

"What if there are fifty righteous people in the cities," Abraham asks. "Will You still destroy them?" No, God answers.

"What if there are forty?" Abraham continues. God says He will not destroy the city if there are forty righteous people.

The dialogue continues through the number ten, after which Abraham asks no further questions (Genesis 18:16-33). Ultimately, the cities are destroyed, and their four righteous residents are saved.

Was Abraham wrong to protest? Should he have kept his mouth shut and simply trusted God's judgment? The text suggests Abraham was right to challenge God even though he was wrong in thinking the cities could be saved, because God had a deeper purpose than winning the argument. God wanted Abraham to challenge Him!

That's why God said, "Shall I hide from Abraham what I am about to do?" (18:17 ESV) *God was testing Abraham's commitment to pursue justice and righteousness.* Would Abraham simply let the two cities fall without putting up a fight? Would Abraham simply accept the world as it is? Or would he envision and work for the world as it ought to be?

Abraham passed the test with flying colors. He had the courage to challenge God in the name of justice and righteousness so that we, his spiritual descendants, have the courage to challenge all the human rulers who seek to replace God's laws with their own. The challenge is as stark now as it has ever been.

God,
Give me the power to stand up for righteousness, even when the world feels stacked against me. Amen.

Chayei Sarah: Genesis 23:1–25:18

Speeding Things Up

Abraham lived to the age of 175. Abraham took his last breath and died after a good long life. (Genesis 25:7-8)

A few years ago an eighty-six-year-old member of my congregation asked to meet with me. "Of course," I replied. I expected him to introduce himself to me so we would not be strangers when the time came for me to officiate at his funeral. (Such meetings are not an uncommon occurrence for a new, young rabbi in a congregation with a significant elderly population.) I was surprised, therefore, when the first words out of his mouth after we sat down were "Rabbi, I'd like you to officiate at my wedding." He proceeded to tell his story.

He had been a bachelor his whole life. Then, after an old friend died, he and the widow began to see each other socially. Now they had decided to get married.

Even as he joked that I could be his grandson, we got to know each other. I met with him and his fiancée. I learned of their vibrant social life, even telling my wife that these octogenarians were getting out much more often than we were. After the wedding, they traveled to Europe and cruised through the Mediterranean.

At his ninetieth birthday party, I made a few remarks and noted that many people begin to slow down in their eighties. This man, however, had decided to speed things up.

In this way, he resembled our biblical patriarch Abraham. As Abraham reaches his nineties, his life seems to take on a new urgency. He engages in extensive negotiations to purchase a burial plot for his wife, Sarah. He finds a wife for his son Isaac. He soon remarries and has another eight children.

Abraham lives with greater urgency in his last days because he knows they are limited. Though living with such urgency requires energy, it also gives energy. Abraham is like the runner who gains speed the farther he goes.

We do not need to be in our nineties to learn from his example. Every moment is precious, and it is never too late to start again.

God,
You give me life. Let me use it wisely. Let me never lose sight of the opportunities for holiness and change abounding around me. Amen.

A Special Song

And the life of Sarah was a hundred and seven and twenty years
(Genesis 23:1a, my translation)

When I was eleven years old, my family moved from Texas to Wisconsin. One of the reasons was a desire for closer proximity to grandparents. The other was more painful: my dad's boss at the medical clinic where he worked had engaged in serious unethical business dealings. The whole clinic was tarnished and had to close. It was a difficult time for my parents.

They hid much of the trauma from me. Yet I do remember my parents playing a particular song in the car and in the house over and over again. The song was Bobby McFerrin's "Don't Worry, Be Happy." It helped them get through a difficult time.

While Bobby McFerrin isn't Jewish, the message of the song certainly resonates with Jewish tradition. Trying to stay happy through traumatic times has sustained the Jewish people. The biblical matriarch, Sarah, is the first example of this truth.

Sarah left her homeland with Abraham. She endured the harem of King Abimelech. She even withstood the near sacrifice of her son, Isaac. Yet, as the biblical text suggests, she found reasons for happiness and hope through it all.

The key to seeing this truth lies in the Hebrew word *chayim*, which is the first Hebrew word in our verse. In Hebrew it has two meanings. The first is "life." That's the translation typically used in this biblical passage. But the word *chayim* can also convey joy, vitality, and excitement. Such a meaning lies closer to the French phrase *joie de vivre*.

This meaning is the sense conveyed in our passage. From a strict literal point of view, we do not need the word. The text could simply say "Sarah lived 127 years." Yet, as the Jewish sages pointed out, the additional *chayim* reminds us that Sarah filled her days with joy.

We will probably not live the same number of days as Sarah, and not all of our days will be filled with joy. Some days will be better than others.

Yet we can follow her example and seek to imbue our days with as much joy as we can. And it never hurts to sing a happy song.

God,
You are with me in moments of pain and of joy, of worry and of comfort.
May I find my hope and happiness with You. Amen.

Keeping Our Cool

Such was the span of Sarah's life. (Genesis 23:1b, my translation)

Our last devotion told us that the life of Sarah was 127 years. Then we read the second part of this verse, and it's completely redundant. What is the reason?

Sarah experienced all of life's ups and downs: she left her homeland with Abraham. She was passed off as Abraham's sister and went briefly into the harem of a king. She suffered through attempts at having a child and grew jealous of her handmaiden Hagar. Finally, she had a child in her old age, yet she died before that child married, made a life for himself, and had his own children. Despite all of these ups and downs, Sarah's character remained unaffected. Her wisdom and righteousness abided through every moment of her life. She had the quality of *hishtavut hanefesh*, a Hebrew phrase meaning, "equanimity, inner calmness, maintenance of an even keel."

Throughout the Talmud (the handbook of Jewish wisdom), the Jewish sages placed a high value on this quality of character. Perhaps it was necessary in facing difficult times of persecution. Perhaps it reflected the emphasis on moderation—Maimonides called it the "middle ground." The Greeks called it the "golden mean."

They also derived its importance from a famous biblical verse from the Book of Micah:

To do justly,
To love mercy,
And to walk humbly with your God. (6:8 NKJV)

These words were inscribed prominently in the sanctuary of the synagogue where I grew up. Commenting on the last verse, the sages asked, "What does it mean to 'walk humbly with thy God?'" It means, they said, "to escort the dead to the grave and lead the bride to the bridal chamber" (see Babylonian Talmud, Sukkah 49b).

What unites these two examples is that they are peak emotional experiences. Accompanying one to the grave can cause grief, while escorting a bride is a great joy. "To walk humbly" in each circumstance is to do so with an inner equanimity and stability, a recognition that life is filled with moments of great happiness and sadness. That is not to say that we should not cry at a funeral or dance at a wedding—far from it. Rather, it is to understand that emotions have their proper time and place. To become endlessly consumed in grief is to lose hope in the future, and to become giddy with joy is to lose touch with the reality of life's difficult times.

God,
Help me see and appreciate Your wisdom through all of life's
ups and downs. Amen.

How to Pick a Spouse

When I [Abraham's servant] say to a young woman, "Hand me your water jar so I can drink," and she says to me, "Drink, and I will give your camels water too," may she be the one you've selected for your servant Isaac. (Genesis 24:14)

The great consultant and writer Jim Rohn is credited with saying that our personality becomes the average of the five people with whom we spend the most time. While this definition is insufficient for capturing our full character, it does remind us that we are influenced by those around us. The people with whom we spend time shape the person we become.

Abraham had this idea in mind when he sought a wife for his son Isaac. Typically in the ancient Near East, arranged marriages served the purpose of tribal relations. A powerful clan would use marriage as a way of building an alliance with another powerful clan.

Abraham, however, is the father of a new religion. His primary concern is not a tribal alliance but a leader who will continue the faith and preserve the values of their new nation.

To find the right person, Abraham sends his servant Eliezer back to his homeland. Eliezer knows Abraham well, and without any instructions from him, he devises a test to find the wife with the ideal character. The trait he seeks is kindness. That is the purpose of the watering test described in our verse. Will she care for the needs of a stranger, or simply focus on her own?

WHAT MATTERS MOST

Let's put aside the cultural prejudices of an ancient society where a father would find a wife for his son, and focus instead on the message of this exchange. Of all the characteristics Abraham would seek in a bride for his son—wealth, physical beauty, intelligence—Eliezer, his servant, knows Abraham prefers kindness.

Perhaps we can take a page from Eliezer's playbook and look for the same qualities in our relationships. And perhaps we can aim to be the kind of person who exemplifies the qualities.

Near the end of his life, Rabbi Abraham Joshua Heschel said, "When I was young I admired clever people. Now that I am old I admire kind people." We don't need to wait until we are old to admire kind people. Let's start now.

Eternal God,
Your kindness is beyond measure. Let me draw from its infinite well so I may bring kindness and generosity to others. Amen.

Toledot: Genesis 25:19–28:9

Esau's Cry

> When Esau heard what his father said, he let out a loud agonizing cry
> and wept bitterly. He said to his father, "Bless me! Me too, my father!"
> (Genesis 27:34)

As children, my sister and I used to fight over who was our parents' favorite. I'm pretty sure most siblings have this argument at one point or another. Sometimes I would say I was the favorite. At other times, when it seemed my sister got something that didn't seem fair, I would charge my parents with favoring her. No parents are perfect; yet my wife and I, and most parents we know, try assiduously not to play favorites.

Unfortunately, our biblical ancestors did not have the same compunction. They frequently played favorites, and the consequences were disastrous. The most memorable example is Jacob's favoring of Joseph, on whom he bestowed a coat of many colors. Yet we have a hard time blaming Jacob because his father did the same thing.

An Original Sin

Jacob's father, Isaac, preferred Jacob's twin brother, Esau. Esau was a rugged outdoorsman, while Jacob was a studious homebody. In contrast, Isaac's wife Rebecca preferred Jacob. Through shrewd manipulation, she succeeded in deceiving Isaac into giving the prized blessing of the firstborn son to Jacob, even though Esau was older by ten minutes.

Why would the Torah contain such a dismal story of harmful parenting? I can think of two reasons: first, the Torah acknowledges our humanity. Some parents do favor one child over another, and by showing what such favoritism can cause, the Torah illustrates our human tendency and warns us of its consequence.

Second, the Torah acknowledges the pain created by a lack of love. In one of its most poignant scenes, Esau cries out in agony. He asks his father if he truly loves him. Does giving the blessing of the firstborn to Jacob mean that Isaac has no blessing left for Esau?

The answer, thank God, is no. God also hears the cry of Esau. His pain does not go unnoticed. Love is not a zero-sum game. Rather, the more we give, the more we get. Ultimately, as they reconcile, Jacob and Esau learn that lesson. So must we.

Loving God,
Shower me with Your love so that I may shower it on others. Amen.

Hearing Is Believing

The voice is Jacob's voice, but the arms are Esau's arms. (Genesis 27:22)

Near my synagogue is a church that always has clever signs. Typically the sign announces the sermon topic for the upcoming Sunday. Recently the sign read "God has unlimited anytime minutes." I wrote it down right away, not only to use it for my own sermon but also because it cleverly captures a profound truth about Judaism. God listens. And so must we.

According to the Jewish sages, *hearing* matters more than *seeing*. The eyes deceive, they taught, but the ear reveals.

The sages' favorite proof text for this truth is the story of Jacob and his father Isaac. Jacob has come before his father to receive the blessing of the firstborn son. He is disguised as Esau. Isaac is physically blind so he cannot recognize the deception immediately. Yet, he still can hear, and he hears the voice of Jacob. His ears reveal the truth; he simply does not listen to it.

For Isaac—and for us—hearing is not just a physical sense. It requires much more. How many of us have listened to someone while we were thinking about something else? How many of us have talked on the phone and read e-mail at the same time? To listen attentively is to be truly present, and it can be a struggle. It often depends more on the heart than on the ears. But it is a struggle worth tackling. Hearing the true sound—not just the echo—opens us up to one another. In hearing one another, we can grasp our vulnerabilities, our dreams, our pain, our joys. We can move past appearances into what truly binds us together.

Hearing also opens us up to God.

A journalist once asked Mother Teresa what she said to God when she prayed. "Nothing," she replied, "I just listen."

"And when you listen," the interviewer asked, "What does God say?"

"Nothing," she replied, "He just listens."

Eternal God,
You hear my innermost thoughts, pains, dreams, and desires. Let me also truly hear others. Amen.

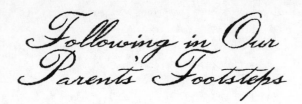

Following in Our Parents' Footsteps

Isaac dug out again the wells that were dug during the lifetime of his father Abraham. The Philistines had closed them up after Abraham's death. Isaac gave them the same names his father had given them.
(Genesis 26:18)

Mark Twain reportedly said, "When I was a boy of fourteen, my father was so ignorant I could hardly stand to have the old man around. But when I got to be twenty-one, I was astonished at how much he had learned in seven years."

We laugh because we know the truth of his quip. As we grow, we tend to appreciate our parents more. We recognize some of their struggles and the challenges we presented, and if we become parents, we may even adopt—consciously or unconsciously—some of their characteristics and habits. Perhaps we like different music and different foods, but we probably share the same expressions and priorities.

I suspect the biblical Isaac underwent a similar evolution. He did not have an easy childhood. His parents moved frequently, and his father almost made him a sacrificial offering!

Yet here we see him digging the wells his father once opened. We are meant to read this verse both literally and figuratively. Isaac is returning to the wells his father once dug, and he is uncovering and bringing forth the teachings his father once planted.

A PERFECT METAPHOR

A well is a perfect metaphor for the teachings of our ancestors. The waters the teachings contain can nourish us. But we have to reach out and bring them up. They are not simply handed to us. The waters may sometimes taste bitter. No parent is perfect, yet they are still essential to life. Without them we would not be here.

Ultimately, the Torah teaches, as Oliver Wendell Holmes put it, that "Every man is an omnibus in which his ancestors ride." Elaborating on Holmes's idea, Rabbi Sidney Greenberg wrote that "We are the product of all those lives which have touched and entered our own—parents and grandparents, brothers and sisters, teachers and friends; those who have bruised us and betrayed us, those who have sustained and strengthened us."[2]

In other words, our lives draw from their many wells. And then we build our own.

God of my ancestors,
Give me the living waters of those who came before me, and help me
nourish future generations with my own. Amen.

Vayetze: Genesis 28:10–32:3

Borrowing Energy

When Jacob saw Rachel the daughter of Laban his uncle, and the flock of Laban, Jacob came up, rolled the stone from the well's opening, and watered the flock of his uncle Laban. (Genesis 29:10)

A friend of mine works out with a trainer. He loves to tell me the different things he does with him. Soon I realized he could do many of the activities on his own, or with a friend he wasn't paying seventy-five dollars an hour.

I asked him why he needed a trainer. He replied, "It's easy. He is full of energy, and when we work out, I borrow some from him. I can do more with him than with anyone else."

Although his insight did not convince me to get a trainer, it did reveal something profound. The people around us can give us energy. There are reasons we spend time with the people we do. One of those reasons may very well be that these people help us be the kind of person we want to be. They give us energy or inspiration or encouragement in doing so.

The matriarch Rachel seems to perform this kind of function for Jacob. He sees her, and then he suddenly has the strength to lift a stone off the well and water her flocks.

The Jewish sages suggested the stone was immensely heavy. Jacob, however, borrowed strength and willpower from Rachel and thereby lifted it. In other words, he did not do it to impress her. He was able to do it because their combined strength was greater than the sum of its parts.

Consider moments when you have done something extraordinary, when you have done something you did not know you could do. What pushed you to do it? Did you picture someone important guiding you on? Somehow *the presence and spirit of another person gives us strength we did not know we had.*

When facing a difficult task, we do not have to do it all alone. We can turn to a friend or partner and borrow some of their strength and will-power. And we can pray with heart and soul and make some of God's strength our own.

God,
You are never far from me. I can find Your presence in the guise of other people, and through them You can bring strength and grace to me.
Amen.

Where Is God?

> He [Jacob] dreamed and saw a raised staircase, its foundation on earth and its top touching the sky, and God's messengers were ascending and descending on it. (Genesis 28:12)

About a decade ago a best-selling book appeared with the title *After the Ecstasy, the Laundry* by Jack Kornfield. This book introduced Zen Buddhist principles, but its title could be used to describe one of the messages behind Jacob's soaring dream.

The Torah says the angels were *ascending* then *descending*. The Jewish sages were careful readers of the text, and they pointed out that the ascending comes before the descending. The text doesn't say the angels went *down and up*. It says they went *up and down*.

This order is a model, the sages said, for the authentic spiritual life. We begin by going up. Like Jacob, perhaps, we have a majestic dream or an experience of faith. It may come while caring for an elderly parent. It may come when we survive a traumatic experience. We may feel a blanket envelope us and a sense of comfort grip us. Simply put, we may have a moment where God is especially present, and we get a glimpse of what we were put here on earth to do.

But then we have to bring that vision to life. *We have to live with a God who is not only present in dreams and visions but in everyday tasks such as doing the laundry.* We need to see God not only when we ascend the ladder but when we descend as well.

In 1929 one of history's greatest Jewish philosophers, Franz Rosenzweig, passed away. He had just finished his literary masterpiece titled *The Star of Redemption*. The book is filled with complex arguments, interpretations, and quotations from thousands of years of Jewish writing. He cites Maimonides, Rashi, Kant, Plato, and dozens of other philosophers. Then, after a thousand pages of ideas for the head, he ends by defining the purpose of the entire book. It takes him one sentence to do so. What were the final words of his book? "Into life."[3]

Eternal God,
As You bless me with eternal life, You call me into this life, giving me the wisdom and strength to make it holy. Amen.

Reminders

Jacob made a solemn promise: "If God is with me and protects me on this trip I'm taking, and gives me bread to eat and clothes to wear, and I return safely to my father's household, then the LORD will be my God." (Genesis 28:20-21)

I once heard a story about a husband and wife who had been married for fifty years. They had a strong, solid marriage, yet they were not particularly affectionate people. Their children, on the other hand, were quite affectionate with their spouses and frequently said how much they loved each other.

After noticing this, the wife said to her husband, "Why don't you ever say to me 'I love you'?" He replied, "I told you that fifty years ago. I'll let you know if it changes."

Even as we laugh, we know his response is insufficient. We cannot express a feeling or commitment once and assume it remains in effect unless we say otherwise. We need reminders, reinforcements, affirmations. Jews say the *Shema*—the prayer proclaiming the oneness of God—three times a day. Many Christians say the Lord's Prayer at least once a day. We need to be reminded of what matters most.

This truth helps us understand this somewhat troubling verse from the patriarch Jacob. On the surface he is expressing a highly conditional faith in God, in essence saying, "*If* You protect me, *if* You ensure my needs are met, *then* You will be my God." That's not the way faith works; we don't set conditions for God. God is not a restaurant chef whose food we can return if we don't like it. God does not run a store where we can return an item if it doesn't fit.

Jacob, however, was not negotiating or setting conditions on God. Rather, Jacob was seeking reassurance from God. Jacob was turning to God in order to renew the strength in himself. Jacob was a like a child getting ready to run a race and looking over at his parents in order to make sure they were still watching. Jacob needed God, as each of us do. We cannot complete the journey all alone.

Rabbi Menahem Mendel of Kotzk once said, "God lives where we let Him in." God lives in us not when we set conditions, but whenever we open our mouths and hearts and remind ourselves of His presence.

God,
You are with me at all times. May I live and act in accordance with Your presence, now and always. Amen.

A Lesson Not Learned

Leah conceived and bore a son, and she called his name Reuben, for she said, "Because the LORD has looked upon my affliction; for now my husband will love me." (Genesis 29:32 ESV)

Like most parents, I want my kids to do well in school. I encourage them, urge them to study, ask questions, and work hard. I also try to use positive reinforcement. Sometimes, however, I go overboard. One day I was so proud of my oldest daughter after she did well on a hard math test that I said, "You're so smart. You're the smartest kid in the school."

My mom, who happened to be at our house at the time and had a career as a teacher, pulled me aside. She told me—as only a mother can—to stop praising Hannah for being "smart."

"Praise her for working hard, for studying, for asking good questions in class. Reinforce her actions, not a label." I did not appreciate the wisdom at the time, but I do now. Praise works best when it focuses on particular actions, when it reinforces good actions and choices.

Unfortunately, the children of the patriarch Jacob did not experience such positive reinforcement. The consequences of this lack of attention are seen in the life of his oldest son, Reuben.

Reuben is a complicated character. He wants to do the right thing but lacks the courage to do so. For example, he persuades his brothers to throw

Joseph in a pit rather than kill him. He plans to go and rescue him after his brothers have gone. But by the time gets there, it is too late. Joseph has been sold to traveling Ishmaelites, unbeknownst to Reuben.

The Torah suggests Reuben never got the attention and praise he needed as a child. His mother, Leah, was unloved by Jacob. She even chose the name Reuben—which means, "Look! A son!"—so that, as our verse suggests, she might get her husband's attention and affection. Sadly, his attention and affection remained elsewhere.

WHAT DOES WORK

Indifference does not breed respect. It breeds anger and apathy. Focused praise, however, brings love and success.

The Jewish sages said the first great rabbi, Jochanan ben Zakkai, used to tell his disciples what their specific strengths were. One had an outstanding memory; one was particularly pious; one was a good teacher of children.

His example offers insight for all of us in our relationships, whether as teachers, friends, spouses, ministers, or parents. We each have unique gifts, and the insight and attention of another can help bring them out.

God,
Let me be a person who notices and brings out the gifts of others. And let me be open to the gifts others nurture in me. Amen.

VAYISHLACH: GENESIS 32:4–36:43

Alone

Jacob stayed apart by himself, and a man wrestled with him until dawn broke. (Genesis 32:24)

A friend who is a priest always asks brides and grooms he marries the same question. "When," he asks, "did you first say to one another 'I love you'? Was it day or night? And what season was it?"

Almost without exception, the answer is at night and in the winter. Now this may have to do with the fact that we are in Chicago, and our winters are pretty long. Yet I think this commonality points to a deeper truth. Our deepest feelings often emerge in the darkness. Sometimes the world obscures and blurs the truth. In the darkness we confront and find it. In the darkness we reveal our vulnerabilities and express our deepest feelings.

Jacob knows this truth. It is in the darkness that he transforms himself. He has not seen his estranged brother, Esau, for twenty years. Their relationship ended when Jacob deceived their father into giving him the blessing of the firstborn son, and Esau pledged to murder him. Now they are about to meet again.

Jacob has left his camp and gone across the river to spend time alone. An angel confronts him, and they wrestle through the night. Ultimately Jacob survives, and the angel blesses him with a new name: Israel. The angel never reveals his own name. The Jewish sages wondered who the angel was and what he represented. The most persuasive answer they gave is that the angel represents Jacob himself. Jacob spent the evening wrestling with his own history, feelings, fears, and hopes.

His new name, Israel, signified a coming to terms with himself. For much of his life, he had wanted to be Esau. He wanted to be his father's favorite. He was willing to deceive, manipulate, and escape in order to get what he wanted. But he could never be Esau. He could only be Jacob. Now he is ready to finally be Jacob, and this changes history, as Jacob makes peace with his brother.

Jacob's story teaches us that we have to resolve the tension in ourselves before we can make peace with others. And, as Jonathan Sacks puts it, "When we are at peace with ourselves, we can begin to make peace with the world."[4]

God,
You make peace in the high heavens. Make peace within and through me here on earth. Amen.

Tough Choices

Jacob was afraid and terrified. (Genesis 32:7, my translation)

My grandfather fought for the US Army for four years during the Second World War. The three years he spent in Europe marked the first time he had left the state of Wisconsin. Those years opened his eyes to a new world and changed his life. They also became the basis for many stories he shared with his grandchildren.

Among his favorite stories was the first time he ate in the soldiers' mess hall. Emblazoned across the walls of the hall was the admonition "Kill or be killed." I shuddered the first few times he told me this story. What an awful, gruesome saying. Did they really want to encourage soldiers to be cold-blooded killers?

As I grew older and studied war and politics, I became less queasy and more understanding of the purpose of the statement. If soldiers like my grandfather were not prepared to kill, they would be killed. Their lives depended on their willingness to kill if the need arose.

A HARSH TRUTH

The biblical Jacob faces this same truth. He has received word that his estranged brother, Esau, is on his way to meet him, and Esau has four hundred men with him. The text then tells us that Jacob is afraid and terrified.

The Jewish sages asked why the Torah says he was both afraid and terrified. It seems redundant. They believed the Torah never repeated a word only for emphasis. Every word conveys something important.

The sages said Jacob was "afraid Esau would kill him" and "terrified lest he have to kill Esau." In other words, Jacob was afraid he might have to kill Esau in order to save his own life.

NO EASY CHOICES

Life doesn't always present us with easy choices. Sometimes we need to do something we never imagined ourselves doing in order to avoid greater harm. Jacob, fortunately, was spared the difficult choice. He and Esau reconcile and share gifts with each other. Yet his story reminds us that while our decisions are not always easy, God is always with us in confronting them.

Eternal God,
You give me the privilege of making difficult decisions. Remind me of
Your abiding presence, and guide me in choosing wisely. Amen.

Vayeshev: Genesis 37:1–40:23

Finding the Fine Line Between Truth and Fiction

All his sons and daughters came to comfort him [Jacob], but he refused
to be comforted. (Genesis 37:35 NIV)

Many little children can be stubborn, but sometimes my youngest
takes it to new heights. Last year we arrived fifteen minutes after a
Baskin-Robbins had closed. She refused to recognize we would not get any
ice cream. "It's not closed!" she pleaded.

"But look at the sign," we said.

"The sign's wrong," she insisted.

When she does not want to go to school, she becomes absolutely convinced school is off that day. Her arguments go beyond simply not wanting
to go to school. She actually convinces herself that school is, in fact, closed.

Such stubbornness drives us crazy. It is also unhealthy. We need to accept the limitations and realities of life. Yet great leaders and spiritual
teachers have always come up against limitations. A fine line separates de-
nying reality from imagining a better world. Sometimes what seems impossible is not.

IS EVERYTHING POSSIBLE?

The Jewish patriarch Jacob knew this truth. This knowledge explains his strange reaction to reports of his son Joseph's death.

Joseph's brothers have brought their father fragments of the coat he had made for Joseph. The coat is dipped in blood and ripped apart. They tell their father that Joseph has been devoured by a wild beast.

He seems to accept their explanation. He rips his clothes and mourns. Yet, as we read, he refuses to be comforted. He says he will die in mourning for his son.

While we can understand his hurt, his reaction raises questions because Jewish law prescribes a specific period for mourning. After a year, we remember a loved one, but the active mourning ritual ends. Jacob states his intent to mourn until he dies.

STAYING STUBBORN

We might say his statement is hyperbole. Jacob couldn't imagine ever getting over this tragedy. Yet the Jewish sages offered a different explanation. They taught, "One can be comforted for one who is dead, but not for one who is still living." *Jacob would not be comforted because he was not convinced Joseph was dead.*

Jacob mourns because he knows his sons have some culpability for Joseph's disappearance. But he refuses to give up hope that Joseph might still be alive. As we learn a few chapters later, his hope bears fruit. Joseph is alive.

Faith does not ask us to believe the impossible. It does challenge us, however, never to give up hope.

God,
You make all things possible. May I have the vision and faith to never give up hope. Amen.

Different Trains

The LORD was with Joseph, and he became a successful man and served in his Egyptian master's household....Joseph was well-built and handsome. (Genesis 39:2, 6b)

In college I once heard a powerful piece of music. Entitled *Different Trains*, it is a rarely performed work by contemporary composer Steve Reich in which he counterposes the sound of moving trains with the orchestra.

The title comes from Reich's own childhood. He was a child during the Second World War, and his parents were divorced. One lived in Los Angeles and the other in New York. Several times a year he rode a train across the country to visit either one or the other.

Reich is Jewish, and he later realized that many of his fellow Jews in Europe were also riding trains during the early 1940s. Their trains led to the death camps. Reich's work juxtaposes the sounds and emotions of each train. One carried a privileged boy across the country to visit his parents. The other carried millions of people to their deaths.[5] The contrasting emotions shock and provoke the listener.

A less stark example of these contrasting emotions is found in this verse of Torah. Joseph's father, Jacob, is mourning his alleged death, refusing to be comforted. Joseph, on the other hand, seems to be living the high life. He is ensconced in the comfortable house of Potiphar, one of Pharaoh's courtiers. He looks "well-built and handsome."

The Jewish sages indicated that he looked good because he spent hours every day pampering himself. What a contrast! Joseph is thinking only about himself and his own needs, while his father suffers because he can think of no one but Joseph.

The Rise of Joseph

Joseph, however, grew and changed. He moved from narcissism to righteousness, from self-absorption to forgiveness. We see this not only in his eventual rise to power and saving of Egypt from famine, we see it *in the way* he reconciled with his father.

Joseph reconciled with his father by forgiving his brothers. Once he had become Pharaoh's prime minister, he could have taken revenge on the brothers who sold him into slavery. He even could have told their father what they did to him.

Joseph, however, cared about his father's feelings. He knew Jacob's knowledge of his sons' wickedness would pain and kill him. Instead, he waited for the right moment when he could forgive his brothers without harming them or his father. He muted his desire for revenge so that he could keep his family together.

Sometimes we think we can't change; perhaps we have fallen into patterns of thinking and behavior. Yet, in the story of Joseph, a narcissistic young man became a model for righteousness and forgiveness.

Eternal One,
Thank You for the power to grow and change and become the person I am capable of being. Amen.

Hidden in Plain Sight

When she realized that he had left his *garment* in her hands and run outside, she summoned the men of her house and said to them, "Look, my
husband brought us a Hebrew to ridicule us. He came to me to lie down
with me, but I screamed. When he heard me raise my voice and scream,
he left his *garment* with me and ran outside." She kept his *garment* with
her until Joseph's master came home. (Genesis 39:13-16, emphasis added)

Occasionally, one word that recurs in a biblical story can hint at an
underlying lesson that does not seem obvious. We have a beautiful
example of this in the incident between Joseph and the wife of his master,
Potiphar.

A courtier to Pharaoh, Potiphar has made Joseph his chief steward. Potiphar's wife—whom the text does not name—is attracted to Joseph and tries
to seduce him. When he refuses, she succeeds in grabbing an article of his
clothing (his *garment*) that she presents to her husband as proof that Joseph
sought to seduce her. Joseph is thrown in prison.

In Hebrew, the word used for "garment" is *beged*. The word *beged* appears
six times during the ten verses describing this incident. It is clearly a word
that cries out for attention.

A clue to its importance can be found in another Hebrew word that
shares the same Hebrew letters. It is the word *begidah*, which means "treach-
ery" or "deception." What is the connection between clothing and treach-
ery? Appearances can deceive. What the eye beholds may hide rather than
reveal truth.

Appearances don't just deceive. Sometimes they can hide what is most important. What we seek most is often hidden in plain sight all around us. Our eyes focus on what is bright and colorful. We see the frosting but miss the cake. We see the smoke but not the fire.

Part of why we read the Bible is to give us a deeper perspective on the world. It helps us see the Eternal amid the everyday.

God,
Help me see and feel your presence, even when my eyes cannot see You.
Amen.

Visions

> The brothers said to each other, "Here comes the big dreamer."
> (Genesis 37:19)

My dad is a therapist and, not surprisingly, his favorite biblical character is Joseph. Joseph dreams. He has visions. At first he is ridiculed for this. His brothers refer to him mockingly as "the big dreamer." Yet it is Joseph's dreams that save his brothers and the Jewish people.

Joseph is not unique in dreaming. Everyone dreams. What distinguishes Joseph is the ability to dream great dreams even in times of crisis. He is in prison when he interprets the dreams of Pharaoh's baker and cupbearer. He is a recently released prisoner—a foreigner, a stranger in a strange land—when he interprets Pharaoh's dreams of the seven thin cows eating the seven fat cows.

Joseph does not let the situation get in the way of the dream. He is not blocked by artificial obstacles. *He lets God speak through him, even when it seems he is the last person through whom God would speak.*

GIVING UP TOO SOON

Too often we give up too early. We let our despair get in the way of our dreams. Those figures, like Joseph, who make history, let their dreams live.

Winston Churchill could have let the overriding power of the German army and the despair of the British people in 1940 destroy his dream of survival and total victory. He did not. Martin Luther King Jr. could have let the persistence of segregation destroy his dream of an America where people would "not be judged by the color of their skin but by the content of their character."[6] He did not.

To dream is not to live in a world of fantasy. It is to imagine a world infused with God's spirit. It is to draw from the energy and goodness God put into our world in order to help make it better.

One of modern America's great rabbis, Sharon Brous, drawing from the work of a great mystical teacher named Kook, wrote, "The whole world stands on our ability to dream great dreams. The whole religious life is designed to remind us to dream, precisely when life threatens to mire us in reality that doesn't match deepest aspirations of our people."[7]

In other words, dreaming is one of the most practical things we can do.

Eternal God,
You gave us the power to dream. Let us dream great dreams with the courage and humility to make them come true. Amen.

Miketz: Genesis 41:1–44:17

Give It Away

> He collected all of the food during the seven years of abundance in the
> land of Egypt, and stored the food in cities. In each city, he stored the
> food from the fields surrounding it. Joseph amassed grain like the sand
> of the sea. (Genesis 41:48-49)

I conducted a wedding once where the bride and groom decided to give away all their gifts. They were not an affluent couple. They could have used the utensils, china, and other household items. They simply wanted to start their marriage off with a feeling of abundance.

Nothing demonstrates our abundance more than generosity. By giving away their gifts, the couple reminded themselves of the gifts of love and companionship that are more valuable than all the others.

On the surface, their generosity and demonstration of abundance seems to stand in opposition to the Torah text cited above. Joseph is not giving away grain; he is accumulating it. Yet, as we know from earlier passages, he is accumulating grain so that he can give it away when the time of famine comes. His accumulation does not serve himself. It serves the people.

We do not need the wisdom of Joseph or the selflessness of the couple I married to appreciate the importance of generosity. Generosity turns us outward. It shifts our focus from the desires of the self to the needs of others. In doing so, it also makes us happier.

The paradoxical truth is that selflessness is selfish. Numerous studies have proved that those who give higher amounts to charity are happier and more satisfied with their lives. In other words, nice guys do not finish last.

Wherever we are on life's journey—whether we have accumulated a lot or a little—we can practice generosity. Jewish law actually requires that a person give enough charity to a beggar so that the beggar himself can give to charity. This law makes no economic sense. It would be more efficient to simply give the beggar what he needs. It does make psychological sense, however, because the ability to give brings a sense of dignity to everyone.

Joseph is the only biblical figure called *hatzadik*, the righteous one. His generosity was part of his righteousness, and it led him to become the prime minister of Egypt. He knew something all of us can experience: giving is the secret to getting ahead.

God of All,
Help me find the strength and love to give to all. Amen.

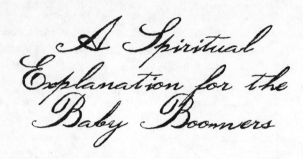

A Spiritual Explanation for the Baby Boomers

Before the years of famine came, Joseph became the father of two sons.
(Genesis 41:50, my translation)

Following the end of the Second World War, America experienced the fastest demographic growth in its history. The phrase "baby boomers" refers to the generation born between 1945, the year the war ended, and 1964. In contrast to this boom, the war years themselves witnessed one of our country's lowest birthrates.

The simple explanation for this contrast is that many men were away at war. Yet we can also glimpse a more spiritual explanation, an insight into human character that can guide us even today.

That insight is found in the Jewish sages' careful reading of our Torah verse. For the sages, no word of Torah is superfluous. Every detail matters. Thus they asked why the Torah tells us that Joseph became a father "before the years of famine came." Couldn't the Torah have just said he became a father? Why did it have to remind us that it happened *before* the famine?

It does so in order to show Joseph's commitment to the Egyptian people. During times of great communal distress, great leaders rarely attend to their own pleasures. For Joseph, one of history's great leaders, a sense of shared humanity during the famine outweighed his own needs for personal joy and pleasure. He could spend the necessary time with his wife and babies only when he was not consumed by the needs and pains of his people.

Joseph's behavior probably strikes us as overly stringent. Do we have to give up all personal pleasure during difficult times? Should the president be barred from taking a vacation?

No. But we can remember, "No man is an island."[8] When the community suffers, we all do. The Talmud puts it this way: "When a community is afflicted, a person should never say that 'I will go to my house to eat, drink and be merry. . . . But rather he should join in the community's suffering.'"

We all know this truth intuitively, even if we sometimes have a hard time explaining and acknowledging it. Perhaps the best way to understand it is to recall a saying attributed to mothers the world over: "A mother is only as happy as her unhappiest child."

Such truth need not depress us. It can remind us to do all we can to build a family and community where joy abounds.

God,
Attune me always to the needs of others so that I may truly help create
a beloved community. Amen.

VAYIGASH: GENESIS 44:18–47:27

What the Bible Teaches

Now, don't be upset and don't be angry with yourselves that you sold
me [Joseph] here. Actually, God sent me before you to save lives.
(Genesis 45:5)

I can still recall the shock and silence in the room. It was an Introduction
to Bible class for first-year rabbinical students. Our professor handed out
a packet of papers, and we began to read through it.

The paper told the story of a young Semitic man and his rise to power in
Egypt. It discussed interpreting Pharaoh's dreams, years of famine, years of
plenty, and a group of brothers reunited. But there was one problem. The
story was not about Joseph. It was not from the Bible. It was an Egyptian
story about a man named Imhotep. He served a pharaoh named Djoser.
He interpreted the pharaoh's dream in order to guard against a seven-year
famine.

Our professor went on to tell us the Joseph story is similar to various
Egyptian legends. It is one of several similar stories circulating in the ancient Near East.

I confess I was not much bothered by the teacher's view. Knowing the
biblical Joseph story has counterparts in other cultures does not mean we
cannot read it as a revelation of God's truth, as an insight into the formation
and values of the Jewish people. The Jewish sages have always believed we

can read the Torah on multiple levels. Why we would read and study it for thousands of years if there was only one exact way to understand it?

READING FOR TRUTH

The Joseph story can be read as an ancient Near Eastern myth about the luck and the rise of a wise outsider who saves Egypt. It can also be read as a story about the unfolding of God's providence. At every moment, God directs Joseph.

When he runs into a stranger who guides him toward his brothers, he is directed by God. When he interprets the dreams of his fellow prisoners and then Pharaoh himself, he is guided by God. In case we do not perceive it, Joseph says it himself. When he reveals himself to his brothers, he says the words, "God intended it for the good."

The same can be true in our lives. From one perspective, our actions may be seen as random and haphazard. From another, they are guided by the hand of God. Like Joseph, we are part of a story much larger than ourselves.

God of Truth,
You give me Your Word. Help me use my mind and heart to discern it.
Amen.

How We Grow

Judah approached him and said, "Please, my master, allow your servant to say something to my master without getting angry with your servant since you are like Pharaoh himself." (Genesis 44:18)

Many researchers suggest our brains stop growing around the age of twenty-five. On the one hand, this is good news, especially for parents of teenagers terrified their kids might not ever grow out of the teen years. On the other hand, this might be bad news, especially for those of us over twenty-five.

Here's my question: when the brain stops growing, does that mean we also stop growing? Faith suggests otherwise. Growth is not just something that happens to our bodies. It is something that happens in our souls. We have more to rely on than the brain. We rely on hearts, and on a powerful force called grace.

Consider the story of the Israelite Judah. Judah begins as one of the spiteful sons of Jacob, the ringleader in selling their brother Joseph into slavery. Judah then has three sons, two of whom die. Israelite law required the widow be married to the next brother, and Judah refuses, fearing that son would die as well.

This refusal leaves the widow—his daughter-in-law Tamar—in shame. She exposes his deceit, and Judah admits his sin. This act changes him. He becomes a leader, willing to admit wrongs, work for good, and push his brothers to grow.

We see this change demonstrated in the fateful meeting between Joseph and his brothers. The brothers do not know they are speaking with Joseph. They simply know him as the Egyptian prime minister. Joseph confronts them with a series of tests to see if they have changed their evil ways.

The most critical and revealing test is Joseph's request to take their youngest brother Benjamin as a prisoner. The brothers know complying with Joseph's request and leaving Benjamin behind would break their father's heart. They refuse, and Judah steps forth and approaches Joseph in our verse, ultimately saying he is willing to take Benjamin's place as a prisoner. For Judah, courage has replaced callousness, and loyalty has overcome selfishness.

Although the Bible does not reveal Judah's age, we know from the ages of his brothers that he is older than twenty-five. He is, according to the Jewish sages, a model for meaningful and lasting change. He finds himself in a familiar situation—he has to defend one of his brothers—and he does not repeat his earlier sin.

We all make mistakes. We all do things we wish we had not. When the opportunity to sin presents itself again, will we act differently? That is the test. Judah passed it. So can we.

God,
You gave me much more to rely on than only my desires. You endowed me with grace and love and the power to renew myself and change.
Amen.

VAYECHI: GENESIS 47:28–50:26

The First Act of Forgiveness

> You planned something bad for me, but God produced something good from it, in order to save the lives of many people, just as he's doing today. (Genesis 50:20)

In 2015 a lone gunman named Dylann Roof murdered nine people at the Emanuel African Methodist Episcopal (AME) Church in Charleston, South Carolina. The nine were among the church members who had gathered for a Bible study. Roof sat with them for an hour, then began shooting.

Soon after he was caught by the police, several family members of the victims announced they had forgiven Roof for his actions. Some in the media and elsewhere questioned and even mocked this act of forgiveness. They used it to caricature people of faith as soft and naive.

In contrast, I greeted the announcement with absolute awe: awe at the faith needed to summon the compassion and willingness to forgive such an act of evil. Forgiveness is one of the great acts of faith. It is counterintuitive, countercultural, and nearly impossible to understand outside of the confines of a belief in a guiding force larger than ourselves.

In this passage, Joseph makes the first great human act of forgiveness recorded in the Torah. According to the Jewish sages, God had forgiven before this, but Joseph was the first person to forgive. He forgave his brothers for having betrayed his trust and selling him into slavery. He did not condone their actions. He did not pretend to understand or explain them away. Rather, he premised his forgiveness on faith. "You planned something bad for me, but God produced something good from it."

Perhaps the best English word to describe the psychology behind Joseph's forgiveness is reframing. Through his faith in a God of righteousness and justice, Joseph reframed the events of the past. He did so because of his faith but not necessarily his faith in his brothers. Even though they seem to have repented, they never apologized directly to Joseph. Rather, he forgave because of his faith in Divine Providence and the desire to build a future untainted by the past.

Forgiveness is a power God gives to each of us. Forgiveness frees us from the prison of the past and points us toward the possibilities of the future.

God,

Grant me the strength to forgive, even when it is terrifyingly hard. Even when I yearn for revenge, remind me of the power of love. Amen.

Young for a Very Long Time

Jacob summoned his sons and said, "Gather around so that I can tell you what will happen to you in the coming days." (Genesis 49:1)

I spent ten summers at an eight-week overnight camp. Looking back, it seems to me like an alternative universe, filled with deep memories and friendships and irreplaceable bonds.

The hardest part of camp was the last day. While we were excited to see our parents, we had to say good-bye to people with whom we had lived for eight intense weeks. There was no social media or video chat then to stay in touch, and even with those technologies, nothing replaces living together. Parting was not only sweet sorrow. It created an aching pain.

The Torah is filled with partings. They, too, display aching pain, and even an occasional bitterness. But they also contain blessings. Perhaps the Torah's most notable parting—Jacob's deathbed statement to his sons—contains a mixture of both. Jacob expresses his love and his anger, his regrets and his gratitude. What is most notable is not only what he says, but his way of saying it.

People who are dying often feel as if they are diminished and weak in the eyes of others. They feel dependent, as if they have become a burden to those who love them. Jacob does not give in to this feeling. Even though he is blind, he insists he knows what he is doing when he blesses one of his younger grandsons before an older grandson, which was not the customary way. Jacob's parting words give him a measure of control and vision in his final days.

Whatever our age, we can model Jacob's grace and vigor. I visited with a ninety-seven-year-old woman in my congregation. She told me a story about her great-grandson. He said to her, "GG, are you old?" And she replied, "No, dear, I've been young for a very long time."

None of us can change our age. But we can hope to be young for a very long time.

God of All,
Life is full of partings. Help me imbue them with love and tenderness.
Amen.

Brothers Who Get Along

Joseph was told, "Your father is getting weaker," so he took his two sons Manasseh and Ephraim with him. When Jacob was informed, "Your son Joseph is here now," he pulled himself together and sat up in bed.
(Genesis 48:1-2)

At the Friday night Sabbath dinner, my wife and I bless our children. We have two girls, so we ask God to make them like our matriarchs Sarah, Rebecca, Rachel, and Leah. When we have nieces or nephews or friends over, we invite parents to bless their boys with the traditional words "May God make you like Ephraim and Manasseh" (Genesis 48:20).

Why these two boys? Many explanations have been offered, but my favorite is that Ephraim and Manasseh were the first siblings in the Torah who actually got along. Think about it: Cain killed Abel, Isaac never met Ishmael until they buried their father, Jacob and Esau battled, and Joseph's brothers sold him into slavery.

Ephraim and Manasseh, however, do not quarrel. And when their grandfather Jacob reverses the custom and blesses the younger one, Ephraim, with his right hand—said to be the stronger one, endowing the recipient with a greater blessing—his older brother Manasseh does not protest. These two brothers break the Torah's violent cycle of sibling rivalry.

In other words, Ephraim and Manasseh are both ordinary and extraordinary. They are ordinary in that they are not patriarchs; they do not start a new religion or speak directly to God. We can relate to them as human beings. Yet they are extraordinary in that they are the first set of siblings in the Torah who get along.

One of the beauties of Torah is that it does not shy away from difficult topics. Anyone with siblings knows we do not always get along. Our similarities magnify our differences, and we are always competing for our parents' approval on some unconscious level, even after they have died.

Ephraim and Manasseh remind us that those obstacles need not be fatal. A few verses before the blessing of the brothers, Jacob uses the word shepherd in describing God's role in his life (Genesis 48:15).

A shepherd cares for his flock. Perhaps siblings are shepherds for one another. They watch over one another, caring as only siblings can.

God,
You are my Shepherd. Imbue my relationships with gentleness and respect. Amen.

White Lies

So they approached Joseph and said, "Your father gave orders before he died, telling us, 'This is what you should say to Joseph. "Please, forgive your brothers' sins and misdeeds, for they did terrible things to you. Now, please forgive the sins of the servants of your father's God."'"

(Genesis 50:16-17)

In the interview for my first rabbinic position, I was asked to teach the search committee my favorite Jewish text. I have lots of favorites, but I decided to use an intriguing passage from the Talmud.

The passage centers on the question of whether it is ever acceptable to tell a lie. The Jewish sages debated the issue, and then posed a scenario: What if you are at a wedding, and the groom asks you, "Isn't my bride beautiful?" If you think she is not, what do you say? In other words, is it OK to lie?

The rabbis ultimately decided we can agree with the groom "because in his eyes, she is beautiful." In other words, the sages permitted us to tell a white lie. They went on to say such lies are permitted only for the sake of peace. We cannot lie to get something or deceive someone. We can only speak a lie if it increases peace and enhances human dignity.

This ruling seems counterintuitive at first. Another verse from the Talmud says, "The seal of God is truth."[9] Yet, for the Jewish sages, nothing was more important than peace: peace in one's family, community, and world.

Sometimes maintaining peace demands saying things or not saying things we wish to say in order to preserve another person's dignity. I often share this story when I counsel couples having trouble with their in-laws, or a bride and groom quarreling over wedding arrangements. Sometimes we have to pretend or agree to something we find disagreeable in order to preserve peace.

Another way to think about when a white lie is permissible is to remember the seminal Torah verse "Love your neighbor as yourself" (Leviticus 19:18). When people come to us needing affirmation or support, we need to consider how we would want them to respond to us if we were in their shoes.

In our passage, Joseph's brothers tell a white lie. They suspect their brother Joseph still seeks revenge on them, and when their father dies, they are afraid Joseph will kill them. So the brothers tell Joseph that their father Jacob ordered them to tell Joseph not to hurt them.

The problem is that no evidence suggests Jacob gave this order. Yet the Bible contains it, reminding us that peace within a family is a fragile and precious thing.

God,
Guide me to seek peace wherever I am and with whomever I am. Amen.

Shemot: Exodus 1:1–6:1

Who Am I?

But Moses said to God, "Who am I that I should go to Pharaoh and bring the children of Israel out of Egypt?" (Exodus 3:11 ESV)

A few years ago a popular book appeared called *The Question Book*. The thesis behind it was that the questions we ask reflect and shape the person we are. Questions are not only about eliciting information. They are about discovering identity.[10]

The idea is not a new one. The Torah itself uses questions to illustrate the human experience and journey. Among the best examples of this truth is Moses's response when God speaks to him from the burning bush. When God speaks to Moses for the first time, Moses asks a question. And it's not the expected one. Instead of Moses asking God about God, Moses asks, "Who am I?"

The question reflects Moses's life journey. He was born an Israelite but raised an Egyptian in Pharaoh's palace. He came from a people of slaves, but he never experienced slavery. He lived in Midian but was called to Egypt. He married the daughter of a Midianite priest, but he was part of the people of Israel. So who is Moses? Is he an Israelite? an Egyptian? a Midianite?

Interestingly, Moses never offers a concrete answer. He never says clearly, as the prophet Jonah later does, that "I'm a Hebrew" (Jonah 1:9).

Yet he answers it through his life. He answers it through his leadership of the people, his challenging of Pharaoh, and his passion for justice and for God.

Like Moses, we may not yet know who we are. We may spend a lifetime trying to figure it out. But we do not declare ourselves into someone; we live ourselves into someone. We discover ourselves through what we do. What draws out our passions, our energy, our love? Where do we feel most alive?

Steve Jobs said famously in a commencement address at Stanford that he could only make sense of events of his life after they happened. The same is true for each of us. We cannot understand our story ahead of time. All we can do is shape who we are through the decisions we make and the actions we take. With God's help, we can become the persons we are meant to be.

God,
You give me the heart to discover who I am. Help me open it with grace.
Amen.

Holy Ground

Take off your sandals, because you are standing on holy ground.

(Exodus 3:5)

I once heard a story about a Jewish leader whom I admire. He was speaking before a large crowd of volunteers. He walked up to the microphone, took off his shoes, and said, "I am standing on holy ground."

The stage on which he stood was not particularly holy. It was a typical platform in a large auditorium. But, he said, the people surrounding him made the space holy. Their deeds, their commitment, their love transformed a normal space into a divine sanctuary.

Believing in this kind of transformation depends on our capacity to create holy spaces. God imbues us with this power. When we pray, when we serve, when we study, we are, according to the Jewish sages, serving as God's partners. We are bringing the holiness of heaven down into the humanity of earth. We reveal God's presence when we act in godly ways.

A great nineteenth-century rabbi illustrated this truth with a trick question for his students. He asked them, "Where is God?" They answered, "Teacher, God is everywhere."

He replied, "No, tell me, where precisely is God?" The students looked confused. They began citing biblical verses showing God's presence fills all of the heavens and the earth. The rabbi kept shaking his head. "No," he finally said. "God exists wherever we let Him in."

Sometimes God feels hidden to us. It's easy to see Him in a beautiful sunset or in the birth of a healthy child. It's harder to see God when a loved one dies or when we encounter an inexplicable tragedy.

Sometimes we try to hear God, and we seem to hear nothing. We feel lost. But God exists wherever we let Him in. Sometimes all we hear is a still, small voice. Sometimes all we feel is the hug of a friend. But God is in these things. And when we let Him in, we realize we are standing on holy ground.

God,
Help me see You whenever I open my heart and yearn
for Your presence. Amen.

How Soon We Forget

Now a new king came to power in Egypt who didn't know Joseph.
(Exodus 1:8)

Every synagogue has a board of directors. Its members serve as the lay leadership of the congregation. They are the equivalent of a group of church elders or governing board. Every synagogue also has a president, who chairs the board, and typically serves as a key partner for the clergy.

The first president with whom I served with was a very wise man. He was in his eighties and had retired from serving as CEO of a major packaging company. He gave me advice I hope never to forget. "No matter what you achieve and how good you are," he said, "you have to prove yourself every day."

At first his words seemed harsh. No matter what we do, he seemed to be saying, it will never be enough. I soon learned that was not his point.

The point was that people do not always have long memories. In our fast-paced global economy, where we put a high premium on competitive skills, we tend to look at our employees and coworkers and ask only, "What have you done for me *lately*?"

THE HARD WAY

The Jewish people learned this lesson the hard way. Joseph had saved Egypt from famine. He had served Pharaoh loyally. His people became loyal citizens.

Then, as the Torah puts it, there arose a pharaoh "who didn't know Joseph" (Exodus 1:8). In other words, he forgot what Joseph and his people did for Egypt. He had no appreciation for the lives saved and the contributions of Joseph's descendants. Instead of seeing the Jewish people as allies and citizens, he saw them as potential traitors. Debasement and slavery followed.

It Matters Today

Hopefully the people who forget our contributions will not inflict such harsh punishments. Yet we all will face times when our actions seem to count for nothing. In such times we need to remember nothing is for naught.

In the Torah, while Pharaoh may not remember what the Israelites did, God does. Indeed the word *remember* is repeated in the Torah dozens of times because God remembers each of us. God records and recalls our deeds. Our memories may be fleeting, but God's endure, now and forever.

God,
Remember me for good, and remember the deeds of my forebearers as a blessing for my own deeds. Amen.

God Is Still Speaking

Moses saw that the bush was in flames, but it didn't burn up. Then Moses said to himself, "Let me check out this amazing sight." (Exodus 3:2-3)

The television-viewing public tends to watch the same stations and news shows over and over. We get comfortable with a certain anchor and angle on the news, and we tune in not only to learn what is happening but also to be confirmed in what we already believe. It's no wonder CNN, Fox News, and MSNBC tend to get the same viewers each night.

This observation is not meant to be a criticism. It is simply human nature, and one confirmed by numerous studies. It takes a major surprise or transformation to break through our natural defenses and change our default approach to the world.

Such a transformation is what we witness in this verse from the Torah. Moses is out in the desert doing his job; he is a shepherd tending his flock. Then a bush begins speaking to him. The bush is aflame but is not consumed. The voice from the bush beckons him to draw near. It is the voice of God, and He is telling Moses to pay attention and listen.

Such an extraordinary occurrence broke through Moses's natural defenses and prepared Moses for the call that was to come. God needed to raise Moses's awareness, to bring about an experience of awe, in order to get Moses to listen and accept his unique task: to lead the Israelites from slavery to freedom.

What happened to Moses can happen to each of us—we can discover our call—but we have to be ready. We have to be open to receive it. We have to be open to awe.

What puts us in such a ready state? Perhaps experiencing the birth of a child, or grasping the beauty and elegance of an idea, or witnessing the hands of God in the acts of human beings—each of these events can open our hearts and heads. We can begin to think about the world around us in a new way.

The key to growing in faith is to remain open to such experiences. Wherever we are, and whatever we are doing, we are always in God's presence. The burning bush, as the Jewish sages put it, is still speaking. We just have to listen.

God,
May my ears be open to the thunder of Your voice and my eyes to the awe of Your presence. Amen.

VA'EIRA: EXODUS 6:2–9:35

What Did Peter Do?

But the LORD made Pharaoh stubborn, and Pharaoh wouldn't listen to
them, just as the LORD had said to Moses. (Exodus 9:12)

When I was a child, I would occasionally misbehave. This happened
most often when my parents were gone, and I was with a babysitter.
My mom would return, and the sitter would tell her what I did.

My mom would then say to me, "Ah, I see Peter was acting up again.
Peter ate the cinnamon rolls. Peter threw the Frisbee in the house. Why do
you have to act like that Peter? Why can't you be Evan all day?"

Somehow, according to my mom, Evan never did anything naughty.
That was the doing of Peter.

Now I recognized that I was Peter. But my mom was not doing good
Jewish theology. We cannot off-load the less positive parts of ourselves onto
someone else. We are born with free will, and our decisions determine our
destiny. Each of us is one unique individual, responsible for all of our actions, not just the ones we like.

THE LIFE OF PHARAOH

We see this truth in the life of Pharaoh. At first, we may think we can
excuse Pharaoh's horrific treatment of the Israelites because God hardened
his heart.

According to the Jewish sages, however, God did not have to do much. Pharaoh's heart had already been hardened. His dependence on slavery had made him incapable of letting the people go.

In effect, his hatred enslaved him. His hatred made him its prisoner, and he could not overcome it. God gives us our freedom, but we are responsible for how we use it. Pharaoh abandoned that responsibility.

Sometimes we are tempted to do so as well. We are tempted to blame our mistakes on others but take full credit for our successes. But freedom and responsibility go hand and hand. The freedom to make choices demands the responsibility to live with their consequences.

BE LIKE MOSES

Our task is to be more like Moses than Pharaoh. Moses experienced pain. He had a speech impediment and had to flee Egypt in the middle of the night. He never entered the Promised Land. But he did not let his heart become hardened by pain and loss. He did not let anger turn into apathy or let frustration become fear; he lived with integrity and an appreciation of freedom. In contrast to Pharaoh, Moses died with "eyes undimmed and vigor unabated" (Deuteronomy 34:7, my translation).

God,
You gave me the freedom to choose a life of responsibility or evasion, freedom or denial. Help me be responsible in making those choices.
Amen.

My Feet Were Praying

Then the LORD said to Moses, "Go and tell Pharaoh, Egypt's king, to let the Israelites out of his land." (Exodus 6:10-11)

One of the twentieth century's great rabbis was a man named Abraham Joshua Heschel. Born in Warsaw, Poland, he made his way through Lithuania to Germany, barely escaping before the onslaught of the Holocaust. He moved to Cincinnati, and then to New York City, where he taught Jewish mysticism and ethics for thirty years.

Among his many achievements was becoming the leading Jewish voice in the American civil rights movement. He formed a close friendship with Martin Luther King Jr., and inspired much Jewish activism. In 1965 he joined Reverend King in the march from Selma to Montgomery, standing out in the front of the march with his head covering and long gray beard. He looked the part of a biblical prophet.

When he returned to New York to teach his seminary classes, the students asked him why he had gone to Selma. It was, he told them, a great act of faith: "My feet were praying."

THE GREATEST STORY EVER TOLD

Heschel's heart and feet drew inspiration from the Exodus story. This story has spawned movements for freedom from Egypt to Selma to Latin

America. It spoke to America's Founding Fathers, who saw themselves as leaving the Egypt of England for the Promised Land of America.

What about this story makes it so powerful? It tells us God is on the side of freedom. God is not on the side of Pharaoh, of slavery, of the means by which we treat others as less than human. God calls on and guides us in our quest to be free, because each of us is made in God's image.

Sometimes we think the concept of freedom was born in America. We believe our Declaration was the first to proclaim that each of us has a right to "life, liberty and the pursuit of happiness." But the idea is much older than America.

It is born in the Torah, in the moment when God breathed life into our ancestors, led them across the sea, and guided them to the Promised Land. It is a gift bequeathed to us. Sometimes we need to pray with our feet to sustain it.

God,

Let me praise You with my feet, my hands, my mouth, and my heart.

Amen.

Bo: Exodus 10:1–13:16

A Heart of Darkness

So Moses raised his hand toward the sky, and an intense darkness fell on the whole land of Egypt for three days. (Exodus 10:22)

As of this writing, one of my two young children remains scared of the dark. At home they have their own rooms. Traveling, however, becomes a problem.

The youngest not only insists on a nightlight, she places about twelve of them at different strategic points throughout the room. It's a constant battle to reach a compromise with the other child, who simply wants to sleep.

While annoying to my wife and me, we know the fear will pass. Many children are afraid of the dark, but almost all of them grow out of it. Darkness is a normal part of life, built into the world.

Is It That Bad?

Why, then, was darkness one of the ten plagues God inflicted on Egypt? It was the ninth plague, and since the plagues were meant to ascend in severity, it purported to be the second-most severe one. This interpretation seems hard to fathom. Isn't a blood-soaked river or lice more harmful than darkness?

The Jewish sages offered a simple but profound answer. The darkness described in the Torah was not only physical darkness; it was a spiritual darkness where, in their words, "a person did not know his own brother." In other words, the Egyptians lost all sense of compassion and empathy. Their hearts became filled with darkness.

DO WE EXPERIENCE IT?

The darkness we experience may not be as severe. But anger and pain can darken our vision. They can lead us to see the worst rather than the best in others. They can cause us to focus on what upsets us rather than what uplifts us. Sometimes, the world looks bright outside but feels dark inside. We cannot escape this darkness alone. We need another person to kindle a fire for us.

In Egypt that was impossible. The darkness was pervasive.

CAN WE ESCAPE IT?

But escaping the darkness is not impossible for us. Our light can kindle another's, because unlike time or money, light is never zero-sum. Lighting another person's candle will not diminish our own.

Darkness may be a plague, but in the words of the great eighteenth-century mystical rabbi, Sefer Yetzirah, "the existence of darkness under-scores light and emphasizes the yearning for it." We yearn for the light, and together can we find it.

Eternal God,
May I always see Your light, and may my light shine together with all
creation. Amen.

The Way We Remember

Moses said to the people, "Remember this day which is the day that you came out of Egypt, out of the place you were slaves, because the LORD acted with power to bring you out of there." (Exodus 13:3)

I almost gave up on my first book. After sending the manuscript to the publisher, I waited patiently. I had labored over that manuscript; I even hired a professional copyeditor to review it before it went to the publisher.

When I didn't hear back, I got nervous. My calls were not returned. Finally, I got an e-mail with the edited manuscript attached. It was not pretty. Lots of sentences had red circles, and lots of paragraphs contained big red *X*'s. Several pages featured a repeated extortion: "Stop telling and start showing. Don't give a lecture. Tell a story."

The lesson hit home. I had been writing like a university professor rather than a rabbi. I was writing only for the mind and not for the heart. The key change for me was to focus on story: to start telling stories to illustrate truths and idea. Stories are remembered long after facts are forgotten.

The Torah reveals this truth subtly and profoundly. Moses wants to ensure that future generations will remember God's deliverance of their ancestors from Egypt. God tells him to write down the story and to celebrate a ritual where the story would be retold every year. That ritual has become known as Passover.

We tell stories. That's how we sustain who we are. It's also how we find out who we are and lead the life we are meant to live. The Scottish philosopher Alasdair MacIntyre wrote in his classic book *After Virtue*, "I can only answer the question 'What am I to do?' if I can answer the prior question 'Of what story or stories do I find myself a part?'"[11]

Faith reminds us of the story of which we are part. For Jews and Christians, we are part of the Exodus story, loyal to a God who redeemed us from slavery. This story ennobles us, reminding us not to take freedom for granted and to work to ensure others have it as well. It reminds us of who our ancestors hoped and dreamed we could be. We sustain that story and keep it alive by retelling it, year after year, to our children and their children for as long as we live and breathe.

God of Life,
You made me part of the story of life. Help me live and retell my story from generation to generation. Amen.

BESHALACH: EXODUS 13:17–17:16

Saying Yes When We Want to Say No

> When Egypt's king was told that the people had run away, Pharaoh and
> his officials changed their minds about the people. They said, "What have
> we done, letting Israel go free from their slavery to us?" (Exodus 14:5)

My friend Michael describes himself as a "recovering people-pleaser." He used to be someone who always said yes. He agreed to just about every speaking engagement or volunteer opportunity offered to him. His family life and health suffered as a result.

He soon realized that saying yes to one thing meant saying no to something else. He determined to change his ways. It has been hard: he still wants to say yes, even when he has to say no.

The Egyptian pharaoh has the opposite problem. He has finally given in to Moses's pleading and agreed to let the Israelites go. He says yes, yet he really means no. Once the Israelites start preparing to leave, he changes his mind and stops them in their tracks.

According to the Jewish sages, however, he never really changed his mind because he never intended to let the Israelites go in the first place. He said yes to Moses to get him to stop bothering him, but he really meant no.

Later events confirm this interpretation. Even when God slays the firstborn sons of Egypt and Pharaoh lets the people pack up and leave, he changes his mind after two days and leads his army in a chase after them.

Now Pharaoh's motives were bad, but sometimes we can make the same mistake even when our motives are good. We say yes when we should say no because we want to build relationships with others. We want to preserve social harmony.

Scientists suggest we have mirror neurons to bond us with the behavior and desires of others. Pleasing others builds group cohesion. But sometimes the desires and assumptions of the group can thwart our own needs. Sometimes another's desire for a yes overwhelms our own need to say no.

The secret to avoid giving in is to start small. Practice saying no to things you could probably easily say yes to, and thereby become acclimated to saying no when the pressure is on to say yes.

We will never achieve perfection in this quest. That's why my friend described himself as a "recovering" people-pleaser. But we can get better at saying what we mean, and meaning what we say.

Eternal God,
Help me make promises I can keep and keep the promises I make.
Amen.

Trusting God

> The whole Israelite community complained against Moses and Aaron in the desert. The Israelites said to them, "Oh, how we wish that the LORD had just put us to death while we were still in the land of Egypt. There we could sit by the pots cooking meat and eat our fill of bread. Instead, you've brought us out into this desert to starve this whole assembly to death." (Exodus 16:2-3)

Teaching about the ten plagues is not easy. Why does an all-powerful God inflict massive pain and death upon the Egyptians? Why do they have to suffer for what Pharaoh has done? And why doesn't God simply free the Israelites and forget about the plagues? Why are they necessary?

None of us can give an absolute answer to this question. God's ways remain a mystery, as stated by the fifteenth-century rabbi Joseph Albo: "If I knew everything about God, I would be God." What we can do is try to understand the lessons of plagues. What possible meaning do they have for us today?

HOW THE PLAGUES FAILED

The answer, paradoxically, is that while the plagues succeed in one area, they fail in another. The primary purpose of the plagues is to free the Israelites from Egypt. They do so by demonstrating to Pharaoh and the Egyptians that the God of Israel is greater than their gods.

The other purpose of the plagues, however, is to instill faith in the

Israelites. It is to spur their trust in God's promise to protect them as they make their way through the wilderness. In this regard, the plagues fail.

No sooner have the Israelites crossed the Red Sea than they begin to complain about not having water. They ask Moses why God led them out of Egypt, just to let them die in the wilderness. They plead for the food and comforts of Egypt.

WHAT KEEPS OUR FAITH ALIVE

The failure of the plagues to achieve this second goal illustrates a lesson for us all. Miracles are great for inspiring, but we cannot depend on them for sustaining.

Faith depends on regular daily habits—things such as prayer, study, and community. We can recall the great proverb "Give a man a fish and he eats for a day. Teach a man to fish and he eats for a lifetime."

Similarly, give us a miracle and we believe for a day. Teach us to see miracles in the everyday and we believe for a lifetime.

God,
Your miracles abound around me. Open my eyes to them
at every moment. Amen.

What God Asks of Us

As Pharaoh drew closer, the Israelites looked back and saw the Egyptians marching toward them. The Israelites were terrified and cried out to the LORD. (Exodus 14:10)

Several years ago I was invited to serve as the rabbi for a trip to Israel. The participants were all men who were active in the Chicago Jewish community. They had chosen a unique name for their group: *Nachshon*.

According to the Jewish sages, *Nachshon* was the name of the first Israelite to walk forward and begin to cross the Red Sea.[12] When he began walking, the sea had not yet split. The Israelites were terrified the oncoming Egyptian army would drive them into it, and they would drown. They called to God, but nothing happened.

Then Nachshon walked into the sea. He walked until the water reached his eyes. Then God split the sea, and the people walked over in safety.

Now we see why the group chose the name *Nachshon*. He exemplified faith and courage. He set aside his fear and acted when no one else would. Without his courage, the Israelites may never have crossed the sea.

GOD DOES NOT ACT ALONE

Nachshon also teaches us a more subtle truth. God does not always act alone. Sometimes we cannot, as the saying goes, "let go and let God." Sometimes God is waiting for us to take the first step.

Figuring out when to act and when to wait is not easy. How did Nachshon know he would not drown? And how do we know the difference between courage and foolhardiness?

The truth is that we will not always know in advance. *What we do know is that God is with us.* We do know God has faith in us, in our ability to act and transform ourselves and the world.

GOD NEEDS US

Perhaps you recall the story about a man caught in a flood. First a friend came by and said, "The storm is coming. Let's go." The man said, "No, God will save me."

Then the flood started, and a boat came by to rescue him. He said, "No, God will save me." The flood soon reached his roof, and a helicopter came by to pick him up. He said, "No, God will save me." He soon perished in the flood.

When he got to heaven, he said, "I had faith. I believed. I prayed. Why did you not try to save me?" And God replied, "First I sent a friend. Then I sent a boat. And finally I sent a helicopter. I did try. You just didn't respond!" Sometimes God calls on us not only to believe but also to act.

Eternal God,
I know it is not easy. Give me the wisdom to know when to stay calm
and when to act. Amen.

Feeling New Strength

Then Moses and the Israelites sang this song to the Lord: I will sing to the LORD, for an overflowing victory! (Exodus 15:1)

After speaking at numerous churches across the country, I have to come to the sad conclusion that Christians sing better than Jews. I know this is not a politically correct observation, but it reflects my experience. (My mom, who sings in our synagogue choir, is an exception!)

One of the problems with Jewish singing is that most of the music is in Hebrew. Since many American Jews do not know Hebrew, they do not always get the words right, or at least in the right order. What frequently happens is that the people in one section of the pews is singing one part of the song, and the people in another section is singing a different part, all at the same time. Putting the words up on a big screen has helped, but the problem seems endemic.

I take comfort, however, in the knowledge that this problem is not new. The Torah tells us that when the Israelites gained their freedom, they burst into song, singing the verses of Torah known as the "Song of the Sea."

The Jewish sages, however, asked an important question. How did everyone know the right words? By conservative estimates there were 1.2 million Israelites crossing the sea. How could all of them have known every word of the song? There was no rehearsal. There were no copies to distribute for everyone to memorize beforehand. Did everyone spontaneously come up with the exact same words to sing?

The answer, of course, is that it was a miracle. God brought the disparate voices together to create a soaring song of freedom.

For the ancient Israelites—and for us—music is the language of the soul. It has the miraculous power to lift us up when we are down and to bring us together when we fall apart. In Judaism we do not just read the words of the Torah. We sing them, adding our voices to the millions who came before us.

In the manuscript for the third movement of one of his final quartets, Ludwig van Beethoven wrote the words *Neue Kraft Fühlend*, "Feeling new strength." When our voices come together in song—elegantly or inelegantly—we feel that strength.

God of Song,
You made me with a voice to sing and praise You. Let me use it with wisdom and joy. Amen.

Yitro: Exodus 18:1–20:23

Introductions

I am the LORD your God who brought you out of Egypt, out of the house of slavery. (Exodus 20:2)

A guest speaker at a church or synagogue or secular program is typically preceded by an introduction. These introductions happen even when everyone knows the person. Even more puzzling, the biographies are typically printed in a handout. Why do we need to take the time for a formal introduction?

One reason may be manners. An introduction shows respect for the speaker. Another more subtle reason is authority. A biography gives some credibility to what the speaker says. It shows his or her message comes from knowledge and experience. We take ideas more seriously when we know their source.

Establishing authority is what God does at the very beginning of the Ten Commandments. "I am the LORD Your God who brought you out of Egypt, out of the house of slavery." These words constitute the first commandment according to the Jewish numbering of the Ten Commandments. (Jews, Roman Catholics, and Protestants each have a slightly different way of numbering the Ten Commandments.)

What is notable about this verse is that it is not strictly a commandment. God is not telling us to do or not do anything. God is simply saying who He is.

By introducing Himself in such a way, God is pushing us to take the following words seriously. But God is also conveying something even more important: *we often live our lives as if the highest authority was ourselves.* We have our iPhones, our iPods, our iPads. It's an "I" life. We find it easy to hear ourselves; we find it harder to hear God.

In making this declaration at the beginning of the Ten Commandments, God reminds us these words come from a being much greater than ourselves. God says, "I am the LORD," because sometimes we think we are. God commands us to listen to His voice because so often we hear only our own.

The paradox is this: by listening to a voice outside of our own, we discover the voice inside us, the voice of conscience, of goodness, of love. And thus we understand that while God spoke the Ten Commandments thousands of years ago, God continues to speak them today.

Eternal God,
Let me hear Your voice with understanding and clarity, now and always.
Amen.

The Back Row

Moses brought the people out of the camp to meet God, and they took their place at the foot of the mountain. (Exodus 19:17)

A few people in my synagogue always sit in the back row. It doesn't matter whether the pews are filled or almost empty. They will sit in the back.

At first this bothered me. Did they sit there just so they could make a quick escape? Or perhaps they like to tune out from worship and take a short nap? But then an older rabbinic colleague suggested neither explanation was likely.

Many people sit in the back, he said, because it brings a sense of perspective. *Not everyone comes to a service to see and be seen. Some come simply to feel the presence of God and feel part of something much bigger than themselves.* Sitting quietly in the back of a large sanctuary brings a perspective of humility and awe, allowing us to appreciate the vast God speaking to and around us.

The ancient Israelites were forced to sit in the equivalent of the back row during the revelation of the Torah at Mount Sinai. Rather than climb the mountain or even go up partway, the Israelites stood at its foot. They could not even touch the mountain on penalty of death.

The traditional rabbinic explanation was that the divine holiness flowing through the mountain was like a powerful electric current. A human being could not withstand its power.

But perhaps the commandment to stand at the foot of the mountain also serves to define the parameters of our relationship with God. We are close to God. Our ancestors heard God's voice at Mount Sinai, and we hear it through God's Word. Yet God is also above and beyond us, transcendent and filling the entire universe.

A beautiful poem by Rabbi Chaim Stern captures this truth, saying, "God, You are as close to us as breathing yet are further than the farthermost star."[13] Prayer is the way we bridge that tension and experience that truth. When we speak to God, God speaks to us.

Eternal God,
May the words of my mouth and my heart reach you in love and awe.
Amen.

Wisdom from Unexpected Places

Jethro, Midian's priest and Moses' father-in-law, heard about everything that God had done for Moses and for God's people Israel, how the LORD had brought Israel out of Egypt. (Exodus 18:1)

The Jewish sages divided the Torah into fifty-four sections. The name of each section is its first significant word. This naming convention leads to some unusual pairings. The Torah portion in which the patriarch Jacob dies is called "And Jacob Lived."

One might think the sages would make an exception for the Torah portion with the Ten Commandments. Couldn't we at least call that section "The Ten Commandments?" The sages disagreed.

The first significant word in the Torah portion in which the Ten Commandments appear is *Yitro*, which is the Hebrew version of the name "Jethro." Jethro is Moses's father-in-law, a non-Israelite and priest in Midian. The foundation of monotheism appears in a section of Torah named for a pagan priest.

Is there something we can learn from this unusual pairing? Indeed. Jethro is not merely a pagan priest. He is a source of wisdom and guidance for Moses and the Israelites.

It is Jethro who tells Moses how to organize courts and resolve disputes among the people. It is Jethro who tells Moses how to remain a leader without burning out. It is Jethro who celebrates Moses's success and gives him the encouragement to continue.

Jethro symbolizes wisdom, and wisdom is not unique to one particular people or religion. Wisdom can be found in all people and all places.

This may sound like common sense, but it is not commonly acknowledged. We tend to be impressed by knowledge or wealth or success. We give greater value to the advice of someone who has a PhD or is a CEO than we do to a sales clerk or a barista. Sometimes we may be justified in doing so. But truth often comes from unexpected places.

One of the first people who told me I should become a rabbi was the custodian at the elementary school I attended in Houston, Texas. He knew before anyone else.

In a section of the Talmud known as "Wisdom of Our Fathers," the sages asked, "Who is wise?" Their answer: "One who learns from all people." Thank God this is true.

God,
Help me learn from all people, wherever I may find them. Amen.

Mishpatim: Exodus 21:1–24:18

God Is in the Details

These are the case laws that you should set before them. (Exodus 21:1)

The first synagogue I served was housed in a building designed by a well-known Chicago architect named Dirk Lohan. His grandfather, Mies van der Rohe, was among the twentieth century's most influential architects.

At one meeting Dirk quizzed us about the size, color, and texture of the candlesticks we used when lighting the Sabbath candles during the worship service. He wanted to make sure they fit with the building architecture. After we answered, he told a story about another architect, Norman Foster, who designed a college building and insisted on managing every detail of the project down to the style and size of the silverware. Dirk then quoted his grandfather. "God," Mies van der Rohe said, "is in the details."

God not only is in the details but also cares about the details. That is the message of this section of the Torah. After the majestic revelation of the Ten Commandments at Mount Sinai, we find a recitation of various laws dealing with cattle, agricultural practices, construction of the Tabernacle, and so on. It seems we move from the sublime to the mundane, like moving right from reading the Declaration of Independence to scouring the provisions of a local traffic code.

A magnificent truth is conveyed here. Righteousness is more than an abstract idea. It expresses itself through the way we live. In other words, the works we do express the faith we hold.

All of us need reminders of this truth. If we tell our children we love them while we are looking at our phones, they may wonder whether we really mean what we say. If we believe every person is created in the image of God, and then we talk down to someone or gossip about others behind their backs, we may rightfully question the firmness of our convictions. We have to act on our vision and on our faith in order to make them real.

The Jewish sages expressed this truth through a wonderful teaching that highlighted the connection between concrete behavior and our highest ideals: "heedfulness leads to cleanliness, and cleanliness leads to purity, and purity leads to abstinence, and abstinence leads to holiness, and holiness leads to humility, and humility leads to the shunning of sin, and the shunning of sin leads to saintliness, and saintliness leads to the gift of the Holy One"[14] To that we can only say amen.

God,

Let me feel Your presence in every detail of life, from the greatest to the smallest and everything in between. Amen.

Why Does the Bible Have Slaves?

When you buy a male Hebrew slave, he will serve you for six years. But in the seventh year, he will go free without any payment. (Exodus 21:2)

Sometimes children ask the question adults are wondering but are afraid or embarrassed to ask. The adults often feel they should know the answer or feel embarrassed by the question.

When I meet with families to discuss this section of the Torah, it is the children who inevitably ask the jarring question: Why does the Torah allow slavery? In the time of this text, the Israelites had just been released from being slaves for four hundred years. God had demanded their freedom, punishing their enslavers with ten horrific plagues. And now they are going to go on and have slaves themselves? How could God allow this?

The answer is not an easy one. The Torah does condone slavery. It takes place in a historical era in which slavery was taken for granted. God frees the Israelites from slavery to Pharaoh, but the Israelites are still servants of God.

But the Torah does teach us that slavery is, ultimately, wrong. No human being should be enslaved to another. We know this truth because there were no slaves in the garden of Eden, which is the biblical version of the perfect world.

Furthermore, the fifth of the Ten Commandments requires that slaves also have complete rest on the Sabbath. Slaves were not inferior human beings. In the Torah they were people who were forced, for whatever reason, to indenture themselves and work for another person.

Why didn't God just abolish slavery after the Exodus? Because human beings were not ready for it. Let us recall that slavery was not abolished in the United States until the Civil War in the 1860s! That's more than three thousand years after the Torah. Realizing our greatest human ideals takes time.

The Jewish sages taught that the Torah is a book of evolution as well as revolution. God moves through human beings, and *sometimes what God desires takes a long time for us to figure out*. As we look around the world today and see the inhumanity still plaguing us, we know we are still trying to figure it all out.

God,
You give me sacred truth. Help me live and act by it every day of my life.
Amen.

Helping Our Enemies

If you see the donkey of one who hates you lying down under its burden, you shall refrain from leaving him with it; you shall rescue it with him. (Exodus 23:5 ESV)

A few years ago I was introduced to the German word *Schadenfreude*. It means "taking pleasure in another person's misery." It's the equivalent of smirking or saying, "He had it coming to him" when something bad happens to someone who did something bad to us.

Schadenfreude speaks to our base human emotions. It is in the same family of feelings as the desire for revenge, which evolutionary psychologists say is one of our most primitive emotions. It is also one of the most destructive. Revenge can create an endless cycle of violence where every act leads to another response.

One of the core purposes of the Torah is to refine and ennoble us as human beings. It is to sustain life rather than destroy it. Thus, Torah helps teach us to channel the energy behind the emotions that hurt us and destroy life into activities that enhance our lives and those of others.

One of the ways the Torah tries to enact this ideal is this particular verse. Our enemy needs our help. Do we give it, or do we walk by with a smile on our face?

The text, as we would hope, demands that we help. Like the parable of the good Samaritan, it urges us to replace hostility with concern. Yet, in their interpretations of this verse, the Jewish sages did not make it so simple.

The sages recognized the temptation of *Schadenfreude*. Part of us wants to walk by and say he is getting his due. That's the part of our brains that neuroscientists call the limbic node.

What counters this limbic node is what the Jewish sages call the *yetzer hatov*, the higher part of ourselves, the human tendency to care and cooperate rather than isolate and destroy. Torah nourishes this *yetzer hatov*. It trains us to listen and follow it rather than to give in to the instinct for *Schadenfreude*.

Think about people in your family or at work who may have hurt you. Would you celebrate if they got hurt themselves? Be honest. Part of us is certainly tempted to do so.

Yet, even three thousand years ago, God taught us we are better than that. A person who loves God cannot simply let another one of God's creatures suffer.

God,
Please give me a heart big enough to love all of Your creatures. Amen.

TERUMAH: EXODUS 25:1–27:19

Gifts Make Community

The Lord said to Moses, "Tell the Israelites to bring me an offering. . . . Then have them make a sanctuary for me, and I will dwell among them."
(Exodus 25:1, 8)

If you've ever attended a professional or religious conference, you are likely familiar with icebreakers. These are games or series of questions meant to help people become comfortable with one another. The questions might prompt you to share a funny story from middle school, your favorite movie, and so on.

I confess I am not a big fan of such icebreakers. While I see their purpose, they seem too superficial. With guidance from the experience of the ancient Israelites, we can learn a much better technique for fostering community. We get comfortable with and connected to one another when we do something together. A shared project brings us closer than any series of five or ten questions ever could.

Moses knows this truth well. The Israelites have just been freed from Egypt. They are still a fractious people, divided into twelve tribes. We know from one of the first incidents in Exodus—where Moses comes upon two Israelites fighting with one another in the field—that they do not always get along. And we know from the stories of Genesis that the conflicts among the tribes have existed from the very birth of their namesakes.

The journey through the wilderness is going to be trying, and the Israelites need the unity of purpose and habits of cooperation to survive. So Moses invites them to work together in the shared project of creating the *miskkan*, the portable Tabernacle, where they gather and pray and experience God's presence in the wilderness.

Each person contributes, with some creating the altar, others putting in the tent pegs, and still others weaving the cloth to adorn the ark. Everyone participates. By the end of the Book of Exodus, the twelve tribes are forced to travel together into one people.

God designed the world to have diversity. We all have different skills and interests. The way to form strong communities is to draw from those differences and use them in shared projects. What unique gifts do you bring to your church or synagogue, your family, your community? When you bring those gifts with you and act on them, you help make each of your communities strong and more enduring.

God,
You designed me for relationship. Let my gifts join with all of creation for Your glory. Amen.

The People Who Lift Us Up

And let them make Me a sanctuary, that I may dwell among them.
(Exodus 25:8 NKJV)

One of the wisest members of my synagogue asked me a challenging question: If God is everywhere, why do we need synagogues? Can't we simply gather in a home or in a park and worship there? Why do we need a special building dedicated to God?

I told him he was right. Strictly speaking, we do not need synagogues. (I don't like to repeat this too much because the synagogue is the source of my paycheck.) But God makes clear from the construction of the first portable sanctuary in the wilderness that they are *not* absolutely necessary.

Notice the grammar in this verse: "make Me a sanctuary, that I may dwell *among them.*" God does not say "make Me a sanctuary, that I may dwell *within it.*" Rather, God says *"among them."* God dwells among the people who gather, pray, and serve together. God lives among people, not within a building.

Now before we go ahead and decide we can find God Sunday morning on the golf course or at the shopping mall where lots of people gather, we need to recall the function of a house of worship. It brings us together for a sacred purpose.

God doesn't need the church or synagogue. But *we do*. Just as the stars are more visible at night, so God's presence can be felt more acutely in a sacred space, a space that makes room for us to encounter the Divine.

And part of making that space sacred is the presence of others. Sometimes we need to pray all alone. But sometimes we also need others to pull us out of ourselves.

I remember one Jewish holiday when the wear and tear of leading the worship service had gotten to me. It was the Day of Atonement when we spend all day in the synagogue. We also fast for the entire day.

The combination of exertion and lack of food had wearied my body and spirit. Then one of my congregants simply put his hand on my shoulder. That gesture gave me new energy. I realized I was not only praying to God, I was helping lift up the prayers of an entire community. That gave me the strength I needed.

God,
Sometimes I hear You directly. Sometimes I hear You in the voices of others. I am so thankful for those voices that You give me. Amen.

The Secret to Wealth

The LORD said to Moses: Tell the Israelites to collect gift offerings for me. Receive my gift offerings from everyone who freely wants to give.
(Exodus 25:1-2)

Many museums in the United States charge for admission. A few, however, ask for a "suggested donation." Now it may seem like a contradiction to "ask" and "suggest" at the same time, but it works. If a sign near the entry says "$5.00 suggested donation for admittance," people tend to leave it. This practice combines the need to maintain fiscal responsibility with community support.

It also speaks to a deeper desire within us: we long to give. Anthropologist Lewis Hyde has written about this desire, which he has seen across cultures. Gift giving, he points out, increases social connections and deepens relationships. Giving creates a new kind of wealth.[15]

God uses this truth to deepen the relationships among the Israelites. Through voluntary giving, they create a community filled with the wealth of holiness.

The Hebrew word for gift—*terumah*—also means "raising up." What is extraordinary about giving is that it not only benefits the recipient but also lifts up the giver. It doesn't just make us feel better; it elevates us to a higher sense of calling. We move closer to God. We also exercise a psychological muscle and develop the capacity to give more. The more we use it, the stronger it becomes.

I saw an example of this truth once in a man who was inspired to donate a Torah scroll to use at a local Christian seminary. He believed Christians should have the opportunity to study and experience a sacred Torah scroll. The joy the students felt in receiving the gift lifted his spirits and gave him a deeper sense of purpose. He donated a scroll to another seminary, and as of this writing, he has donated more than twenty Torah scrolls to Christian seminaries around the world.

The Torah, we notice, does not tell us the exact gift to make. That is our task. We need to ask ourselves what we can give. What gifts can we give to our family? What gifts can we give to our community? What gifts can we give to our church or synagogue? What gifts can we give to our world?

When we discover the answer to those questions, we will know, regardless of how much money we have in our bank account, how it to feels to be truly wealthy.

God,

You shower me with gifts. Help me shower them upon others. Amen.

Tetzaveh: Exodus 27:20–30:10

A Need to Be Needed

Tell all who are skilled, to whom I have given special abilities, to make clothing for Aaron for his dedication to serve me as a priest.

(Exodus 28:3)

Before rabbis had cell phones, Jack Riemer used to phone his congregation every day whenever he was out of town. He wanted to see if any issues or needs had arisen. "I had a tinge of sadness," he writes, "whenever nothing had happened. I realized I wasn't always needed."[16]

His honesty is refreshing. Those of us in the "helping" professions—clergy, counselors, doctors, and so on—love to be needed. Some *need* to be needed. But one of the lessons of the Torah is that no person is indispensable. Only God is.

The Torah teaches this lesson in a subtle way. This week's Torah portion is notable for what it lacks. Moses is nowhere to be found. This section of the Torah is the only one from Exodus through Deuteronomy where the name of Moses is not mentioned. The focus is on Aaron and the responsibilities of the high priest.

Would we feel insulted or belittled if we had been in Moses's shoes? Do we feel a need to be needed? Are we disappointed when our kids or friends or our aging parents do not really need our assistance or advice? If so, we can take a little inspiration from Moses.

Moses, it seems, is relieved when God gives him a break. He needs the time to recharge and regain the perspective and vision necessary for leadership. As we read earlier, the people's complaining had drained him, and he was forced to get advice from his father-in-law Jethro to relieve his burdens.

Moses didn't always need to be needed. Neither do we. In fact, what we need more than anything is to be ourselves and to lead with our unique gifts.

A story is told about a Rabbi named Zusya. As he was dying, he was trembling with fear. His students asked him, "Reb Zusya, why are you afraid? Are you afraid God will ask you, 'Zusya, why were you not more like Moses?'"

"No," Zusya responded, "I am afraid God will ask me, 'Why were you not more like Zusya?'"

Eternal One,
Everything I need, You have given. May I always know that is enough.
Amen.

One in Heart

Summon to you your brother Aaron and his sons from among the Israelites to serve me as priests—Aaron and Aaron's sons, Nadab and Abihu, and Eleazar and Ithamar. (Exodus 28:1)

As a younger sibling, I always thought my parents favored my older sister because she was more mature and responsible. She claims she always thought they favored me because I was younger. Despite these feelings and our significant differences in skills and interests, we get along well. The key has been respect and acceptance.

Our relationship is an exception to those in the Torah. The Book of Genesis, for example, is filled with sibling rivalry. Cain murders Abel. Ishmael is banished when Isaac is born. Jacob and Esau are estranged for twenty years. It is not until the Book of Exodus that we see a healthy sibling relationship where they successfully work together. It is the one between Moses, Miriam, and Aaron.

These siblings have good reason to be jealous of one another. God chooses Moses to lead the Israelites out of Egypt. On first glance, it seems Aaron is the more qualified. He is articulate, whereas Moses has a speech impediment. He is also older and has been in Egypt while Moses has been in Midian. Choosing Moses as the leader may have felt to Aaron like a slap in the face from God. And Miriam saved Moses's life and assured he grew up in Pharaoh's palace.

Yet, despite God's choice, when Moses returns from Midian and the brothers reunite, Aaron and Miriam greet Moses warmly. Aaron becomes Moses's mouthpiece, saying, "Let my people go" to the pharaoh.

Despite being chosen by God to lead the people, Moses has reason to envy Aaron. God makes Aaron the high priest, a position the sages believed Moses desired. And Aaron is beloved by the people while Moses is feared.

Yet, Moses and Aaron accept each other and work together in extraordinary ways: They stand united when confronting Pharaoh. They address the Israelites as one voice. They perform miracles together. Their strengths complement each other.

Sibling rivalry is not inevitable. In fact, through Moses and Aaron, the Torah conveys the truth that siblings can attain a relationship of unique depth.

When Moses and Aaron meet with the pharaoh, the Torah occasionally refers to them with the singular pronoun "he." The rabbis have suggested they had become one in heart. Their creative tension produced a unique whole.

God,
You link us together. May we accept and strengthen one another. Amen.

What Our Clothes Say About Us

Make holy clothing that will give honor and dignity to your
brother Aaron. (Exodus 28:2)

A few weeks after I began serving my first synagogue, an older member came to see me. "Rabbi," he said, "I'd like to take you shopping. You are a wonderful speaker and teacher, but you don't look like a rabbi. We're going to get you a blue blazer, some gray pants, a navy suit, and three white shirts."

Initially I was a bit upset. I thought my clothes were fine. Sure, my shirts were occasionally wrinkled, but did that really matter? I was a spiritual leader, not an attorney appearing in court or an investment banker trying to impress clients. But I decided to indulge my congregant and go.

Sure enough, a week later we went to Joseph A. Bank, and he helped me start a new wardrobe. If my tie was ever out of place, this man (or one of his friends) was sure to fix it for me. Soon, dressing the part of the rabbi became habitual, and my friend would always give me a smile when he saw me in a freshly pressed suit.

My initial hesitation sprang from wrong preconceptions. I thought clothing was unimportant. Yes, in the grand scheme of things, the clothes probably do not matter to God. But they matter to us. Our clothing matters to the way we are perceived, and whether we like it or not, people judge our seriousness by our dress. The kind of environment we create is shaped by the clothing we wear. The kinds of feelings we spark in others depend in some measure on the way they see us.

This truth helps explain the detailed descriptions of what the Israelite priests wore. Their clothing reflects their office. It radiates holiness and devotion to God. It reminded the people of the tasks to which the priests had dedicated their lives. It did not convey superiority; it fostered holiness.

Unlike that of ancient Israel, the trend of our culture is against formality. We prefer comfort to tradition. Perhaps, however, we are losing something in the process. Perhaps holiness is not only what we say and feel. Perhaps it is also found in the way we present ourselves in the world.

God,

Clothe me with dignity and grace so I may bring myself and others closer to You. Amen.

Ki Tisa: Exodus 30:11–34:35

Accepting Our Brokenness

When he got near the camp and saw the bull calf and the dancing, Moses was furious. He hurled the tablets down and shattered them in pieces at the foot of the mountain. (Exodus 32:19)

The writer and teacher of teachers, Parker Palmer, writes much about the dangers of perfectionism. In one telling insight, he reminds us that "Wholeness does not mean perfection: it means embracing brokenness as an integral part of life. Knowing this gives me hope that human wholeness—mine, yours, ours—need not be a utopian dream, if we can use devastation as a seedbed for new life."[17]

This is one of those statements that, when said in a church or synagogue, leads people to say, "That's right" or "I'm convicted." It also captures the meaning of one of the Torah's central acts of brokenness.

Moses has descended from the top of Mount Sinai. He carries with him the two tablets of the Ten Commandments. In his absence the Israelites have built and are dancing around a golden calf. When Moses sees them, he throws the tablets to the ground, shattering them forever.

The conventional way of seeing this act is that Moses broke the tablets because of his anger and frustration. But the Jewish mystics see this act differently. They suggest Moses's shattering the tablets was the beginning of healing, of reconciliation between God and the Israelites.

The people had sinned. They had lost the faith that came through the wholeness and the perfection of the original set of tablets. Now they would have to find it in the shattered fragments. Those fragments were not to be discarded and left on the mountain. They became the broken pieces through which the Israelites crafted a renewed faith.

How many of us have found faith out of brokenness? How many of us have gone through a failure or a traumatic experience and have gathered the shattered remnants of our earlier faith into a more beautiful, enduring whole?

That's what happens when Moses shatters the tablets. He shatters the illusion that faith is easy and that we will always have the strength to be perfect believers. That is a truth to comfort and guide us.

God,
You made me human. I struggle to believe. Give me the strength to do so and accept me in my brokenness. Amen.

The Blame Game

> So all the people took out the gold rings from their ears and brought them to Aaron. He collected them and tied them up in a cloth. Then he made a metal image of a bull calf, and the people declared, "These are your gods, Israel, who brought you up out of the land of Egypt!"
>
> (Exodus 32:3-4)

Children have the ability to come up with the most amazing excuses. Whenever we hear that our oldest daughter has been caught talking in class, my wife and I look at each other and start speculating on the excuses she will offer up.

"My friend needed help opening the right app on her computer" or "I was cold, and I was asking my friend if she was too." And, of course, the classic, "My friend started talking to me first."

Of course, it's not just kids who make excuses; we all do. It goes back to Adam and Eve when Adam blames Eve, Eve blames the serpent, and we are left to speculate about whom the serpent blamed.

Moses's brother, Aaron, also plays the blame game. Moses left him in charge when he went to speak to God atop Mount Sinai. When Moses returns and sees the people dancing around a golden calf, he is furious with Aaron. He asks how he could permit such idolatry to happen.

What is Aaron's response? "Don't get angry with me, sir. You know yourself that these people are out of control" (Exodus 32:22).

In other words, don't blame me. You know how pushy these people can be. They made me do it. Moses immediately jumps into action, figuring out how best to respond to the incident and get the Israelites moving again. His action stands in stark contrast to Aaron's inaction.

How would you have responded if you were in Aaron's shoes? It's easy for us to say, "I would have taken the blame and responsibility. I would have asked for forgiveness and done something to fix the situation." Perhaps. But it is much easier to be a Monday morning quarterback than to make the call on game day.

Perhaps the most plausible lesson we can learn from the litany of biblical examples of blaming others is that it comes naturally to us as human beings. We are often inclined to avoid responsibility when things fall apart. Victory has a thousand champions, the saying goes, while failure has none.

Yet, if we can watch our tendencies and our language—if we can try to shift our initial impulse from thinking, "It's not my fault" to "What can I do to fix it?" we will become a little more like Moses.

God,
It is easy to play the blame game. It is harder to accept responsibility.
Help me live up to the best within me. Amen.

Write It Down

The LORD said to Moses: "Write down these words because by these words I hereby make a covenant with you and with Israel." (Exodus 34:27).

In the 1930s and 1940s a musicologist named Alan Lomax traveled the American South. He sought to write down the folk songs and ballads played by blues musicians and bluegrass singers in rural areas. Most of this music had been passed down through the generations and had never been written down. This man wanted to capture it to ensure it was not lost to history.[18]

Why did he feel the need to write down these songs? Because those rural communities were collapsing. People were leaving them and moving to bigger cities. Children were not staying in the same town as their parents. If the music was not written down, it would be lost to history.

The sacred texts of Judaism and Christianity experienced the same phenomenon. They were originally transmitted orally. The Torah, in particular, was transmitted orally for hundreds of years. No one knows exactly when it was first written down, but most scholars agree it was sometime around 586 BCE, when the Babylonians conquered Judea. Many Jews moved to Babylonia, and parents were not sure their children would return. The Torah needed to be written down in order to survive.

This process repeats itself throughout history. The Talmud, which was originally the Jewish sages' oral commentary on the Torah, began orally and was written down during the collapse of the Roman Empire. Other commentaries moved from oral transmission in the classroom to book form when communities were persecuted and forced to migrate.

The Torah itself urges us to maintain an interplay between the written and spoken word. That's what sermons continue to do. That's what Bible study continues to do. And that's what God intended.

In commenting on the verse above, the great Jewish sage Rashi wrote, "We write down the written Torah. But we are forbidden from writing down the Oral Torah." The Oral Torah consists of the conversations we continue to have every day with one another and with God.

God,
I give thanks that You reveal truths to us through the words on the page, the words of our mouths, and the words in our hearts. Amen.

Vayakhel: Exodus 35:1–38:20

Crowd Mentality

Moses gathered together the whole Israelite community and said to
them: These are the things that the LORD has commanded you to do.
(Exodus 35:1)

The 1990s comedy *The Waterboy* features an interesting character with no
name. This character—played by *Saturday Night Live* star Rob Schnei-
der—shows up at all the football rallies. He perfectly mimics the spirit of
the crowd. When everyone is cheering for the water boy, played by Adam
Sandler, he screams and shouts loud hurrahs. When everyone is booing and
upset, he screeches and hurls insults. His behavior is totally shaped by the
sentiment of the crowd.

This character is an extreme demonstration of what can happen to each of
us. We get carried away in a crowd. Mobs exert an enormous psychological
power. Good people lose their self-restraint. Rage can be unleashed among
the calm, or even a voluble group can become silent. Our rational minds can
be hijacked by the powerful feeling of the group.

The dangers of this truth are well known. Nazi Germany used mob psychology to transform a Western nation into a barbaric machine of hate. Like
much of life, however, there is good alongside the bad. Group psychology
can also be channeled for the good.

Moses shows us the way to do it. He knew the power of the group feeling among the ancient Israelites. The exact same word used in our Torah verse—*vayahkal*, "to gather"—is used earlier in the Bible to describe the Israelites coming together to build and dance around the golden calf.

So now Moses gathers the people for a new purpose: building the Tabernacle. Like the golden calf, the Tabernacle will serve as a symbol of God's presence in their midst. Unlike the golden calf, however, the gathering is not about idolatry. Rather, it symbolizes commitment to God's word. It brings people together for good.

We should be careful about the groups we join. They can draw from our best instincts or our worst desires.

Eternal God,
When we gather for Your purpose, allow Your justice to prevail. Amen.

Meaningless Questions

The winged heavenly creatures spread out their wings above, shielding the cover with their wings. The winged heavenly creatures faced each other toward the cover's center. (Exodus 37:9)

My mentor Rabbi Arnold Jacob Wolf was fond of telling a story. He had taken his two sons, ages nine and eleven, to Israel. He set up a time to meet with the renowned philosopher Martin Buber, with whom Rabbi Wolf had studied. He was eager for his sons to meet him.

When they got to Buber's home, Arnold introduced Buber. He then asked the children if they had any questions for the great theologian. They could have asked about the meaning of life or the reality of God. Instead the boys asked him how the telephone system in Israel worked. Buber then spent almost an hour explaining all the details to them.

Buber believed God dwelled in relationships, in the way we speak to and seek to understand one another. He could have chided the children for their simple question, but he lived what he wrote. He lived with people where they were.

His most influential book, *I and Thou*, argued that God is the third party in such relationships. Whenever two human beings relate authentically, God dwells among them.

Buber was drawing on an idea implicit in the Torah. The heavenly creatures referenced in the verse above were sculptured angels that stood on either side of the ark of the covenant. Legends abound about their appearance and purpose. What we see here, though, is a simple description of their posture toward one another. They faced each other. They did not look up into the heavens, and they did not look away into the horizon. They looked at one another.

Faith fails us if it only leads us to look upward. It also must guide us to look toward one another, to build relationships of depth and meaning and responsibility.

Heavenly Father,
Help me spend my life reaching out and loving others as You would have me love them. Amen.

One Word

Do your *work* for six days, but the seventh day should be holy to you, a Sabbath of complete rest for the LORD. (Exodus 35:2, emphasis added)

Sometimes one word or one sentence can change the world. Think about Martin Luther King Jr.'s "I Have a Dream" speech. Or Moses's words to Pharaoh "Let my people go." Entire movements and journeys sprung out of those words.

We see a less dramatic yet equally significant example of this truth in our Torah verse. The critical word here is *melakah*. Its literal meaning is "work." It answers a critical question the ancient Jewish sages posed. We know, they said, that work is forbidden on the Sabbath. But what constitutes work? How do we know what "work" is and what it is not?

Think about it. For some people, writing is dreadful work. For others, however, it is a great joy. For some, gardening is hard labor. For others, it is a joyful hobby. How do we know the meaning of work?

The answer lies, again, in the word *melakah*. What is revealing is the way it is used in the Torah. The Torah tells us that work on the construction of the Tabernacle was forbidden on the Sabbath. The Hebrew word that is used for this kind of work is *melakah*.

That prohibition gives us a working definition of *melakah*. It refers to any kind of labor necessary for the construction of the Tabernacle. These include hammering, sawing, metal making, carrying, kindling of fire, and so on.

With this definition in mind, the Jewish sages went a step further. They classified each of these actions in broad categories and said all the types of labor in each category were forbidden. They came up with thirty-nine categories, and hundreds of actions fall within those categories.

Thus, this one word—*melakah*—is the sole basis for all the traditional practices of the Sabbath. It shaped the way Jews, and then Christians, understood the Sabbath as a day when shops were closed and little business was done.

Appreciating the power of one word can change our behavior. Perhaps you have a word in your family that shapes your thoughts or behavior.

In my family, I say the word *gratitude* at a meal or when we are having a conversation, and my kids know to shift their behavior. My grandfather used to use the word *tact* among the staff in his office to remind them how to relate to patients. Words shape our thoughts, our actions, and our lives.

God,
Help me use my words for honor and praise, and never for shame and insult. Amen.

PEKUDEI: EXODUS 38:21–40:38

Celebrate Good Times

When Moses saw that they in fact had done all the work exactly as the
LORD had commanded, Moses blessed them. (Exodus 39:43)

Every Jewish worship service has a time for prayers for healing. People
mention the names of loved ones and friends who are ill. At my synagogue we have also introduced a time of prayers for celebrating. People
stand up if they wish and name something good that has happened to them
or someone they love over the past week. I confess it is my favorite part of
worship. Faith brings us comfort, but it can also help us elevate and sanctify
the moments of happiness.

Sometimes in the rush of life, we forget to celebrate. Something good
happens to us and we think either (a) Things are good so something bad will
probably happen soon; or (b) OK. What's next?

That's not healthy. Celebrating helps move us forward and build community. When the Israelites finished constructing the Tabernacle, they paused
and celebrated. Moses lifted up his hands and blessed the people. The Torah
does not mention it, but I would bet the people had a big party to celebrate
the construction of God's home on earth.

Celebrating not only marks sacred moments, it also gives us the energy
and direction to improve. Rabbi Jonathan Sacks tells an extraordinary story
of a school he visited during his tenure as chief rabbi of Great Britain. The

school population had fallen from one thousand to five hundred. And only 8 percent of students achieved decent grades. The morale in the school— among students, parents, and teachers—was abysmal.

The principal asked Rabbi Sacks for advice. "I want you to live one word," he said. "Celebrate."

She sighed and replied, "You don't understand—we have nothing to celebrate. Everything in the school is going wrong."

"In that case," Rabbi Sacks replied, "find something to celebrate. If a single student has done better this week than last week, celebrate. If someone has a birthday, celebrate. If it's Tuesday, celebrate." She seemed unconvinced, he noted, but promised to give the idea a try.

Eight years later, the principal wrote a letter to Rabbi Sacks describing what had happened. "Exam results at high grades had risen from 8 to 65 percent. The student population had risen from five hundred back to one thousand." And, as Rabbi Sacks notes, "She had just been made a Dame of the British Empire for her contribution to education."[19]

Did all that happen just because they started celebrating? Probably not. But the acts of celebration shifted perspective. They unleashed a new attitude that spread through school. Morale matters. A single finger, a rabbi wrote, can block the sun. A single smile can bring it back.

God,
Help me celebrate good times in gratitude and joy. Amen.

Holy Work

The Israelites did all of the work just as the LORD had commanded Moses.
(Exodus 39:42)

During my first year as a rabbi, I had the chance to get to know a very accomplished man. He had been a state supreme court justice, highly regarded attorney, philanthropist, grandfather, and great-grandfather. He became ill, and I spent many hours with him at the hospital and then the rehab center.

One day we were talking and he said to me, "Rabbi, I'm going to die soon. What does it all mean?" I replied, "Well, you've done so much with your life. You're leaving such a legacy for your family." He said, "Stop it. Yes, OK, I've done a lot. But be honest...in five or six generations, no one will know my name. None of what I did will really matter. What's it all about?"

Rabbinical school had not prepared me for such a question. And I honestly don't remember what I said in reply. But I do remember the way the question pushed me to go deeper into the theology and beliefs I professed. It pushed me to confront the meaning of eternity, the meaning of the legacy of the life we live. It pushed me to look anew at those immortal words from Ecclesiastes, "Vanity of vanities. All is vanity" (1:2 ESV).

Is that true? Not according to the way Jewish sages read our Torah verse. The verse says "all of the work" of the Tabernacle was complete. It could have just said "the work" of the Tabernacle was complete. The phrase "all of the work" signifies the eternal importance of the Israelites' work.

The labor of the ancient Israelites did not just change their world. It drew from the past, built for the present, and shaped the future.

So does our work. It links us with the labors of those who came before and will come after us.

So often we think of just the Sabbath as the holy part of the week. But God also says "six days you shall labor" (Exodus 20:9 NKJV). That work is commanded by God as well. We can make all of life holy. And when we work with purpose, we leave a legacy not just in what we accomplish, but in the way we lived.

God,
May my work bless You as You bless my work. Amen.

Give Me the Details

These are the accounts of the dwelling, the covenant dwelling, that were
recorded at Moses' instructions. They are the work of the Levites, under
the direction of Ithamar, Aaron the priest's son....The total amount of
the gold that was used for construction of the whole sanctuary, gold
from the uplifted offerings, was twenty-nine kikkars and seven hundred
thirty shekels in weight, measured by the sanctuary shekel.

(Exodus 38:21, 24)

If you have received requests for charity, you may have noticed a one- to
five-star ranking assigned to the charitable organization. These rankings
evaluate the way a charity spends its money. Does most of the money raised
go to the people or groups in need? Or does much of it go toward admin-
istrative costs?

We need these rankings because we want to give to organizations that are
dedicated to causes we care about, but we also want to make sure our gifts
are not wasted. We want to make sure that even the most sacred groups are
responsible for being good stewards.

Moses and the ancient Israelites were no exception. Even Moses—God's
servant who spoke with God face-to-face—has to provide an accurate ac-
counting of the gifts and materials used to construct the Tabernacle. He is
thorough and detailed in his report.

Yet Moses's example here teaches us about more than just honest ac-
counting. It also tells us the spiritual life is not about living in clouds. It
is not a hazy sense of some spiritual power. *Righteousness requires attention to*

detail. A sacred life is a life of careful attention. It is one where we examine our actions thoroughly and in detail.

A few years ago, when I was rereading Henry David Thoreau's classic *Walden*, I encountered a paragraph echoing this Torah verse. In describing the material used to build his home in the woods, Thoreau tells us he spent "$8.03 1/2" on wooden boards. Then he tells us the exact amounts he spent on lime, nails, bricks, and so on.[20]

Thoreau is not doing this just to bore us. He is sending us a message. A faithful life does not squander our gifts. It accounts for them. It cares for them. It is responsible for them.

Today this approach can feel countercultural. Our culture says we have earned what we have, and it's ours to do with it whatever we please. In the end, however, what we have does not belong solely to us. It belongs to God. We are but stewards, and a good steward pays attention. A good steward is mindful. A good steward cares for God's creation.

Eternal God,
Help me be a good steward of the gifts You have set aside for me and all of Your creation. Amen.

Notes

What Angels Can't Do

1. Martin Copenhaver, "Didn't I Wash Your Feet?" United Church of Christ online, www.ucc.org/daily_devotional_didn_t_i_wash_your_feet (accessed October 28, 2016).

Following in Our Parents' Footsteps

2. Sidney Greenberg, "Using Other People's Years," sermon seminar, 1980, http://collections.americanjewisharchives.org/ms/ms0603/ms0603.090.008.pdf (accessed October 28, 2016).

Where Is God?

3. Franz Rosenzweig, *The Star of Redemption* (Madison: University of Wisconsin Press, 2005).

Alone

4. Jonathan Sacks, "The Blessing of Love (Naso 5776)," Rabbi Sacks online, www.rabbisacks.org/blessing-love-naso-5776/ (accessed September 15, 2016).

Different Trains

5. Christopher Fox, "Steve Reich's Different Trains," in *Tempo*, no. 172 (March 1990): pp. 2–8, www.jstor.org/stable/945403?seq=1#fndtn-page_scan_tab_contents (accessed October 28, 2016).

Visions

6. Martin Luther King Jr., "I Have a Dream," speech delivered at the Lincoln Memorial, Washington DC, August 28, 1963.

7. Sharon Brous, "Defying Despair: Why I Believe," *The Huffington Post*,

www.huffingtonpost.com/sharon-brous/defying-despair-why-i-bel_b_135229.
html (accessed October 19).

A Spiritual Explanation for the Baby Boomers
8. John Donne, "Meditation XVII. Nunc lento sonitu dicunt, morieris,"
Devotions upon Emergent Occasions (1959), https://www.ccel.org/ccel/donne/
devotions.iv.iii.xvii.i.html (accessed October 28, 2016).

White Lies
9. Babylonian Talmud, Tractate Shabbat, 55a

Who Am I?
10. Mikael Krogerus and Roman Tschäppeler, *The Question Book: What
Makes You Tick* (New York: W. W. Norton, 2014).

The Way We Remember
11. Alasdair MacIntyre, *After Virtue: A Study in Moral Theory* (London:
Bloomsbury, 2013), 250.

What God Asks of Us
12. Babylonian Talmud, Tractate Sotah, 37A.

The Back Row
13. Chaim Stern, ed., *Gates of Prayer* (New York: CCAR, 1975), 180.

God Is in the Details
14. Mishnah Sotah, chap. 9, v. 15.

The Secret to Wealth
15. Lewis Hyde, *The Gift: Creativity and the Artist in the Modern World*
(New York: Vintage, 2007).

A Need to Be Needed
16. Jack Riemer, a sermon shared on Facebook.

Accepting Our Brokenness
17. Parker J. Palmer, *A Hidden Wholeness: A Journey Toward an Undivided
Life* (New York: Jossey Bass, 2009.)

Write It Down

18. Bio of Alan Lomax, www.culturalequity.org/alanlomax/ce_alanlomax_bio.php (accessed October 28, 2016).

Celebrate Good Times

19. Jonathan Sacks, "Pekudei (5774)—Celebrate," Rabbi Sacks online, www.rabbisacks.org/pekudei-5774-celebrate/ (accessed October 28, 2016).

Give Me the Details

20. Henry David Thoreau, *Walden* (Hollywood, FL: Simon and Brown, 2011), 34.